MW00910858

People Are Saying ...

Word-Weaver

My lifelong friend and fellow author Jeanne Halsey spins a yarn so beautifully that you long to snuggle deep into the cashmere afghan, sip a steaming cup of *Earl Grey,* and linger in the cocooning magic. She weaves the words 'til you taste the colors – and they are scrumptious!

A voracious reader, seasoned teacher and master story-teller, she has faithfully lit the flickering lamps of the ever-winding artistic path. Now she smiles her mysterious smile while reaching out to gingerly clasp trembling hands: *"Come, let me show you the way of words,"* she beckons.

Personally, I plan to sign up for every road and bunny trail! I wouldn't miss the adventure if I were you!

~ *Reba Rambo McGuire*, Contemporary Christian Music Singer/ Songwriter, Author of *Follow the Yellow Brick Road,* Pastor of *The River at Music City* Church in Nashville, Tennessee, U.S.A.

Watch Out, World!

Jeanne's book will have a major impact on the professional writer, the would-be writer and the individual who wants to be inspired to write even if it's for their own personal enjoyment.

I'm particularly thrilled as a teacher for her thoughts on keep a daily journal, as I believe strongly in journaling as I pray and study God's Word. I am very appreciative of her mention of my small part in this book by being an encouragement to her. As her [former] pastor, I'm excited this Godly woman has taken pen in hand ... watch out, world!

~ *Rev. Robert A. Seymour*, Senior Pastor of *Royal City Community Church* in New Westminster, British Columbia, Canada

Team Effort

Christ For All Nations contracted Jeanne Halsey to assist us in a project that entailed the review and research of **Reinhard Bonnke's** volumes of written materials, for the purpose of editing and drafting his first daily devotional book. Her work also involved extensive Scriptural cross-referencing, and the careful collation of his resources, to help pull together the initial draft of this particular undertaking.

Jeanne Halsey did a very commendable job. She worked diligently with our team and maintained a positive attitude throughout her phase of the development of this work, **Mark My Words.** We sincerely appreciate the role she played and the contribution she made to the team effort, which went into the successful completion of this endeavor.

~ *Rev. Tom Henschke*, former United States Director, *Christ For All Nations,* Orlando, Florida, U.S.A.

Three Gifts

I have always loved Writing! Life's events, never-ending "to-do's" and busy schedules caused me to bury this hobby and passion, so much so that I had forgotten what joy it brought to my life.

Recently I received three amazing blessings from God. Blessing 1: I met Jeanne Halsey, gifted author, encourager and friend. Blessings 2 and 3: *The School of Creative Christian Writing* and *The Legacy of Writing* – both taught and written by Jeanne. These three blessings have given me confidence and a realization that my passion for writing is more than a hobby – it is a God-given gift that He intends for me to use for His glory. I am most grateful to God and to Jeanne for helping to rekindle this passion.

~ *Angela Lewis*, writer-in-training; Bellingham, Washington, U.S.A.

Challenged to Write

I attended the 2006 class of the *School of Creative Christian Writing*, having no other expectations than learning something new. By the end of the class I was challenged by Jeanne Halsey to write a book. The Lord gave me the subject and the title of my book, *"Forging Ahead for God."* It is the biography of my father who was the pioneer-missionary to the West Coast of Vancouver Island, British Columbia, and a man of great faith.

~ *Darda Burkhart*, Author of *Forging Ahead for God*; Lynden, Washington, U.S.A.

She is an Accomplished Writer

If you are considering enrolling in Jeanne's writing class, I highly recommend you do so. She equips you with the skills to begin writing, and has an excellent teaching style. Not only does she encourage you, she also motivates and teaches all that is required to begin a possible future for you as a writer. I am so grateful to have experienced her expertise in the writing field, as she is an accomplished author. *Thanks, Jeanne!*

~ *Joyce Mulder*, novice writer; Lynden, Washington; U.S.A.

The
Legacy
of
Writing

Jeanne Halsey

ISBN 978-0-557-41753-7
Second Edition

The Legacy of Writing by Jeanne M. Halsey (1953-); second Edition. Copyright © 2012, 2003, 2010; revised 2012; ISBN 978-0-551-41753-7. Published by *ReJoyce Books,* an imprint of MASTERPIECES IN PROGRESS Publishing House. International copyrights secured; all rights reserved.

ReJoyce Books, in loving memory of **Joyce A. Gossett** (1929 ~ 1991)

This book is protected under the Copyright Laws of the United States of America. No part of this book may be reproduced or transmitted in any form or by any means, electronic or mechanical, including photocopying, recording, or by information storage system, in any manner whatsoever, without express written permission of the Publisher, except in the case of brief quotations embodied in critical articles and reviews.

Unless otherwise indicated, all Scriptures are taken from the *New King James Version of the Holy Bible;* copyright 1979, 1980, 1982 by *Thomas Nelson, Inc.;* all rights reserved; used by permission. *The Message* by Eugene H. Peterson is copyright 1993, 1994, 1995 by Eugene H. Peterson; published by *NavPress;* all rights reserved; used by permission.

Cover Photo: ***The Moses,*** a sculpture by the Italian Renaissance artist **Michelangelo di Lodovico Buonarroti Simoni** (1475-1564); housed in the Church of San Pietro in Vincoli, in Rome, Italy. Unless otherwise indicated, all photos are from the Halsey Family Archives.

For more information, contact:

ReJoyce Books
4424 Castlerock Drive
Blaine, Washington 98230
United States of America
www.halseywrite.com

Table of Contents

Foreword by Don Gossett 15

Acknowledgements 17

Dedication 23

Preface 25

Chapter One: **The Legacy of Writing** 29
▸ Y2K, the Millennium Bug
▸ Who Do You Like?
▸ The Words of an Experienced Writer: Cecilia Holland
▸ The Birth Experience
▸ Lesson One

Chapter Two: **The Power and Permanence of WORDS** 41
▸ Writers Love Words
▸ Writers Are Communicators
▸ World-Wide Impact
▸ Lesson Two

Chapter Three: **Start With the End in Mind** 51
▸ The Running Story
▸ The Writer's Tree
▸ How?
▸ Trade Secret
▸ Establish Incremental Deadlines
▸ Lesson Three

Chapter Four: **Target Your Audience** 65
▸ Professor Phil
▸ Sarah and Reinhard
▸ Alex and SBS
▸ Christianese
▸ Lesson Four

Chapter Five: **Getting Started** 79
▸ Writer's Block
▸ Writing Keys

▸ The "Hands" Experience
▸ A Single Idea
▸ Lesson Five

Chapter Six: **The Unique Gift of Ghostwriting** 95
▸ I "Act It Out"
▸ Team-Work
▸ It Ain't Rocket Science
▸ Does It Bother Me?
▸ Don't Put It Off
▸ Lesson Six

Chapter Seven: **Make an Appointment** 103
▸ Key-Word: SELF-DISCIPLINE
▸ Teamwork
▸ My "Little Secret"
▸ Lesson Seven

Chapter Eight: **Multiple Styles** 111
▸ Mini-Script
▸ Back to School!
▸ Emphasize Your Strengths
▸ Give and Get Credit
▸ Lesson Eight

Chapter Nine: **Publications CHALLENGES** 129
▸ The Enemy is Watching
▸ Stillbirths and Adoptions
▸ My Terms and Conditions
▸ A Handful of Suggestions
▸ Lesson Nine

Chapter Ten: **Publication POSSIBILITIES** 137
▸ Subtitles
▸ Lesson Ten

Chapter Eleven: **Poetry in Motion** 147
▸ Constructive Criticism
▸ Background

- ▸ Work in Progress
- ▸ First Draft
- ▸ Feedback
- ▸ Final Draft
- ▸ *Exit the Dragon*
- ▸ Lesson Eleven

Chapter Twelve: **God Versus Ego** 163
- ▸ Hot Hands

Supplemental: **Assignments** 167
- ▸ The Classroom Assignment
- ▸ The Homework Assignment

Open House 169
Resources 175
- ▸ Letter of Agreement

About the Author 179
Other Titles 181

Foreword
By Don Gossett

The Lord has abundantly blessed me to be the father of five children. Each of them possesses special giftings. For Jeanne, I long ago recognized she was "my writer." From the time she was very small, she had the urge to put things on paper. It was no strain for her to compose stories and other creative pieces.

Through the years, the Lord has used Jeanne's gifting for writing to impact nations – as editor of international magazines, author of books, Christian dramas and comedies, and other items. I too am a writer and author of more than 100 books. Jeanne has capably assisted me in writing and re-writing publications that have enhanced their presentations.

To Jeanne, I say: *"Daughter, you have made me proud to see and experience your talents in this field of writing. God has made you a blessing to multitudes. I commend your new book, and value your expression in the printed page. Love always, Dad."*

Rev. Dr. Don E. Gossett
Author of bestseller *"What You Say Is What You Get"* and *"My Never Again List"*

Rev. Don E. Gossett (photo April 2011)

Acknowledgements

The first person I want to acknowledge is my older brother **Michael Leon Gossett,** who is actually responsible for me learning to read at the age of four (and subsequently, learning to love writing). Michael is two years my senior; therefore, when he enrolled in public school at age 6, he brought home his schoolwork – especially those "learning to read" books – and he willingly shared them with me. While he was in First Grade at school, learning to sound out his letters and make them into words, I was at home ... also learning to sound out my letters and make them into words – and soon entering into the enchanting world of books! *"Thank you, Michael, for your lifetime of support."*

Above: Michael Gossett
Below: Donnie Gossett

Then there is my younger brother **Donnie Gossett.** Donnie is two years my junior, and he does what I cannot do: he writes **songs.** Well, yes, I can write *lyrics* for a song, but he writes **both** the music and the words. Donnie and I composed one song together, *"Introduction to a Friend,"* while on a weekend camping trip when we were both teenagers, but Donnie has since written (and co-written) and recorded dozens and dozens of witty, poignant, sometimes hilarious, catchy, rocky songs. Because I enjoy all kinds of writers and writing styles – from the clever people who create commercial advertising, to the heartfelt poet who writes a love-song – I salute my "baby brother," who is also a talented software "code writer."

There are two wonderful people I have known since my early teens, and since they have watched me grow up, they felt free to ask me to volunteer to do something very special for them – even if it was way out of my comfort zone. Naturally, with such trust in each other, I willingly

Rev. Dennis White

complied. I am referring to **Pastors Dennis and Esther White,** who were Senior Pastors of *Nairobi Pentecostal Church* in Nairobi, Kenya, East Africa.

In February 2000, I traveled to Nairobi to augment the ministry of my father, I learned immediately upon my arrival, on a Tuesday morning, that they had scheduled me to teach a class of Creative Christian Writing at their church campus on the next Saturday morning. Therefore, I obediently spent most of those interim days dredging up ancient memories of "teaching" and "creative writing" techniques, and eventually devised a hand-written outline, which their church staff (especially dear **Sarah**) typed, photocopied and had ready to distribute to the class.

More than a hundred students showed up for that single, all-day class. I was glad that I did not learn until **afterwards** the mix of people who were in the class: housewives, university professors, untried writers, students, popular newspaper columnists. Overall, the class was a success because I did what burns strongly in my heart: I was able to **motivate** people to become writers, to understand the importance of the legacy of writing, and to speak uniquely from their own hearts through their written words, writing for the benefit of their own culture and people. If Dennis and Esther had not felt comfortable to ask me to extend myself for *that* class, *this* book probably would not exist today.

In this book you will learn an important key to writing: *the target audience.* As I wrote this book, I had two specific people in mind as my targets: a dear friend from church, **Dorothy Barker,** who has privately shared her heart's desire to learn to write ... and my nephew **Jeremy Wiebe,** who also aspires to use his gift of writing in his ministry and career. I hope this book will guide and inspire both of them, and they will flourish as writers themselves.

Many others have contributed to my belief in the fact that I am a writer today, and for that I am deeply grateful. Some are excellent writers themselves, some have simply been "good listeners" to my heart:

Judy Vanderhoof Godwin ... Suzanne Kauss ... Maggie Kinney ... Shara Pritchard Nixon ... Reba Rambo-McGuire ... Kim and Anne Ryan. Later in this book I will explain something about my former pastor Rev. Bob Seymour, for to him I also owe a debt of thanks.

Of course I acknowledge the invaluable input I have received from my loving family: Don Gossett, my father who "gave" me his writing talent ... his wife Debbie, who initially critiqued this book ... Marisa and Ken Nyman, my beautiful younger sister and her husband, who both love to read and can be trusted to give honest evaluations. My various nieces and nephews: Michael's children Victoria (now Froelich) and James Gossett ... Donnie's sons Brandon (a fine writer too), Jordan and Justin (both developing songwriters) ... Marisa's daughters Vanessa (now Pedersen), Jessica, Rebekah (who has been a special helper at The School of Creative Christian Writing), and Samantha Nyman – all these young people who good-naturedly performed in the little family skits I created for holiday meals and family get-togethers, so their encouragement is also appreciated.

Finally, there are our fantastic daughter Jennifer and her husband Patrick Freeman, and their beautiful children Kristian and Ava ... our outstanding son Alexander Halsey and his lovely wife Cherry, and their precious children Jude, Aja and Hayley ... and, of course, my husband R. Kenneth A.J. Halsey – these are the people who make my life worthwhile.

Already so many persons in my immediate and extended family have exhibited their own flair for writing and publishing; I strongly believe this is a God-gift that He imparted to our family, and we all

(From top) Don and Debbie Gossett ... Ken and Marisa Nyman ... Victoria (née Gossett) Froelich and James Gossett ... Brandon and Kelsey Gossett, Justin and Jordan Gossett ... Samantha, Jessica, Rebekah Nyman, and Vanessa (née Nyman) Pedersen

have the responsibility to use that gift as He enables us. The world that I know **will** be different because this legacy is alive in my bloodline!

There are two others who deserve recognition here. The first you will read about in the Dedication; the Other you will read about in the last chapter.

Jeanne Halsey
Birch Bay, Washington
December 2012

My Extended Family, in 2011. (Back row, left to right) son-in-law **Patrick Freeman** ... daughter **Jennifer** (née Halsey) **Freeman** ... daughter-in-law **Cherry** (née Beck) **Halsey** ... nephew-in-law **Jared Pedersen** ... niece **Vanessa** (née Nyman) **Pedersen** ... niece-in-law **Kelsey** (née Greave) **Gossett** ... husband **Kenneth Halsey** ... nephew **Brandon Gossett** ... nephew **Jordan Gossett** ... **Jeanne Halsey**, holding granddaughter **Hayley Halsey** ... nephew **Justin Gossett** ... grandson **Kristian Freeman** ... Kristian's girlfriend **Claire Nelson** ... son **Alexander Halsey**. (Front row, left to right) granddaughter **Aja Halsey** ... grandson **Jude Halsey** ... granddaughter **Ava Freeman** (holding my hand).

Dedication

Since I first wrote this book in 2000, a cataclysmic event took place in my life: I lost the biggest fan and encourager of my writing, my beloved sister **Judith Anne Gossett.** Judy was born 28 July 1952 and I was born 15 August 1953; we were always the best of friends as truly blood-sisters can be. When she was 9 and I was 8, I was promoted out of my Third Grade class at Bose Road Elementary School into her Fourth Grade class ... and from that time onward, people thought we were twins – which was amazing since we were so unalike in physique and personality.

Judy (right) and me (circa 1955)

Judy became my protector, my advocate, my social organizer. I really needed her because she was so popular and outgoing while I was totally a wallflower. She "made" her friends like me too, or else! While we had some elements of typical "friendly rivalry" regarding academics – which I believe spurred both of us to truly excel in our schoolwork – we were primarily sounding boards for each other as we began to discover our unique gifts and prepare for "real life." From those early years, I always took my writing to Judy for her critique, which I could count on to be accurate ... and all throughout my life, she continued to be the greatest encourager of my gift.

On 24 November 2003, I was working on my computer at my home in Blaine, Washington, when I received an urgent phone call: Judy had just been taken to Emergency at Peace Arch Hospital in White Rock, British Columbia (about 15 minutes across the international border). She was suffering extreme abdominal pain, and the doctor ordered immediate tests. I dropped my work and went straight to the hospital ... and for the next 18 days, I was with Judy every possible moment.

I was clutching Judy's hand when the first doctor finished examining her and said she suspected cancer. I stayed with Judy throughout the days and nights as she battled the unexpected diagnosis and the horrendous pain. I talked her through the agony of dialysis as they tried to stabilize her failing body. I regularly ministered Communion to her (usually using the hospital's cans of grape juice and packages of crackers). And I understood her completely when, early on the morning of 11 December, she grasped my arm, locked me with those intense green eyes, and said forcefully, "Jeanne, I want to get out of here. Help me get out of here. Jeanne, do you understand? I want to die. Help me get out of here." She was ready to go Home – and she needed her loved ones to understand that, and to let her go.

We did the only thing we knew to do: we worshipped our sovereign Heavenly Father with song and in prayer, thanking Him for the wonderful life He had given our beautiful sister, and releasing her with trust back to Him. We sang with her – and maybe sang *for* her – as her spirit approached the Gates of Heaven ... and then, as her spirit slipped out of her earthly body, those Gates swung open for her and she passed through into the presence of God. We were left behind as the Gates closed again, until our own times come.

I miss my sister more than words can express. I vow to continue being the best writer I can be, never wasting the gift God has given me ... and somehow I think Judy is *still* proud of my writing. Even as I write this, I can still hear her voice saying, *"Press on, Jeanne, keep pressing on."* So **I dedicate this book to the memory of Judy Gossett, my beloved sister.**

Judith Anne Gossett ~ 1952-2003

Preface

If you have worked your way through the entire Acknowledgements, you already know that I have been strongly influenced to write this book because of Dennis and Esther White. But my practice of motivating people to write goes back much before 2000. I started teaching Creative Writing with children at a private Christian school (also teaching – somewhat poorly, I should add – Graphic Arts); then later expanding to informal "classes" with adults, usually in the form of conversations, letters and occasionally as public lectures. Although I attended college (majoring in Theatre, minoring in Journalism – go figure!), I really do not have any special training to be a writer – I simply **am** a writer! And I am very willing to share with others what I have learned and experienced, to boost their skills and increase their productivity.

In 1985, my husband's employer transferred our family from the Pacific Northwest to the southern heartland of Dallas, Texas. After we settled in, I expected to look around for a part-time job, and even signed up with a "temp" agency to work occasionally as an executive secretary. To my astonishment, an old friend from back home – who just happened to also be a Media Consultant for a major Christian ministry based in Dallas – phoned one day and asked, "Jeanne, do you think you could run a monthly magazine?" The current Managing Editor was abruptly retiring due to a difficult pregnancy, and on short notice they needed a competent person to fill her shoes.

The skyline of Dallas, Texas

At the interview with the ministry's vice-president, we discussed the opportunity, I presented my (few) credentials (while realizing I was being considered more for the weight of the recommendation of the consultant ... and on the basis of my maiden name, the daughter of a famous author), then he offered me the job ... which I accepted on the

Some of my staff at the monthly Christian magazine; on the far left is my administrative assistant and genius **Dawn Hard.** (1985)

spot! An important adage that pertains to nearly all aspects of Life: *"It is often not **what** you know but **who** you know."*

That night, my husband and children and I went out for pizza to "celebrate Mom's new job." I became the Managing Editor of a monthly Christian magazine, with an international subscription base of 300,000. I learned most of what I needed to know from the administrative secretary on staff in my new department, **Dawn Hard,** and by drawing on vague memories of working with my high school weekly "newspaper." Certainly I could write – and "ghostwriting" is one of my special God-given talents – but I did not know much at all about publishing a monthly print magazine. The "on-the-job-training" – courtesy of Mrs. Hard, primarily – was intense and even daunting ... but we got that first issue to press on time. From that point onward, it was total joy for me!

I used to walk briskly into the office building every weekday morning, greet the staff warmly and professionally, quickly review my messages and calendar with Dawn, give whatever instructions were necessary, step into my private office, gently close the door behind me ... and deliriously dance and jump for sing, singing, ***"I get to write today ... and I get paid to do it!"*** My employers were kind and tolerant of me, and I still thank them for that opportunity of a lifetime which just "fell into my lap." It was a productive season of writing for me ... and I am addicted to the smell of printer's ink to this day.

My love of Writing comes from a strong love of Reading. As a child, I would perform my household chores with a book in one hand and the handle of the vacuum cleaner in the other (do you think those carpets ever got very clean?) ... or have a book propped up on a nearby table while ironing (no, I never ruined any shirts) ... or a book wedged in the windowsill while washing dishes – it is no wonder I still dislike housework! My sisters will attest to me hiding under the blankets at night and reading by the very, very inadequate light of the electric blanket control – it is no surprise today I wear corrective lenses for my poor, abused eyes. My husband will also agree that his rest has often been disturbed by my reading in bed with the nightstand lamp turned on – *"Just to the end of this chapter, honey,"* I always say – when he would much prefer we were both asleep.

(Above) **Marisa** and me, about 1965.

(Below) **Marisa,** my daughter **Jen** and me (2010).

One key to being a good writer is to have a vivid imagination. Ask any of my siblings and they will tell you I had the most colorful imagination of our entire family – maybe in the entire world! – and could spin stories out of the air for hours at a time. Patient **Marisa** (my younger sister, with whom I shared a bedroom during much of our growing-up years) had to listen to my "Technicolor™ dreams" every morning as we were dressing for school. She

often said, "My dreams were black-and-white and boring compared to Jeanne's." But my imagination continues to enrich my life and heart with its own brand of excitement and delight, adding drama and color to every-day life.

Now, you can discern by the length of this Preface that I really enjoy writing, and I could go on and on. But the purpose of this book is to motivate **you** to write, so let us begin.

NOTE: The original goal of this book is to augment the in-class training when I conduct *The School of Creative Christian Writing.* However, it can also be used effectively for private, individual study. My only caution is that, as quickly as possible, you acquire some fellow Writer(s) with whom you can exchange ideas and discuss these principles.

Chapter One: *The Legacy of Writing*

Y2K, the Millennium Bug

At the beginning of 1999, the entire world was in a turmoil about the soon-approaching "crisis year" known as *Anno Domini 2000.* Predictions of disaster – natural and man-made – were rampant, especially the fearful possibility that our world (as we know it) would come to a cataclysmic end, particularly regarding technology. *"All the computers in the world will crash at midnight"* ... *"Airplanes will fall from the skies"* ... *"People will no longer be able to take hot showers because the power companies will malfunction"* (that one **really**

Y2K, the Millennium Bug

bothered me!) ... and on and on went the dismal predictions of disaster. Millions of dollars were spent by governments on the all-consuming *Y2K, the Millennium Bug,* searching for ways to prevent its destructive bent.

In retrospect, it was **the most significant non-event of the millennium itself.**

As 1999 ticked around the calendar, people began to think more optimistically about the coming new millennium, and they began to review the passing millennium as a whole – one thousand years of recorded history to dissect. Early in December 1999, my husband and I watched a two-night television special which featured a "countdown" of the one hundred most significant people of the second millennium, from AD 1000 to 2000. These people were selected by an impressive panel of scholars, scientists, sociologists – professionals who could speak knowledgeably about these historic persons and their impact upon Earth and humanity, and therefore their recommendations could be taken seriously. Kenneth and I watched most of the countdown with interest, often agreeing with their choices, sometimes thoroughly surprised, occasionally completely disagreeing – but with a roster of one hundred

people (and in some cases, a small group of people counted as one unit, such as "the Beatles"), they had a lot of ground to cover: everyone from artists and explorers of the Renaissance period, to politicians and scientists of the late 1800s and early 1900s, to entertainers and athletes of the twentieth century.

As the final Top Ten approached, we both speculated about whom the producers might choose as "the most significant person" of the second millennium. So many people had such world-wide impact: **Billy Graham** ... **Elizabeth I of England** ... **Martin Luther** ... **Neil Armstrong** ... **William Shakespeare** ... **Christopher Columbus** ... **Joan of Arc** ... so many others! Of course, during the countdown, some of these people were certainly nominated and honored, but the Number One Most Influential Person of the Second Millennium was ...

... **Johannes Gutenberg,** the inventor of the moveable-type printing press. He brought *knowledge* to Mankind's daily world because now books could be written, produced and distributed *en masse,* no longer restricted to the libraries of wealthy men and the hallowed halls of elite churches. He inspired **writers** to become free to be prolific. The rate of international literacy skyrocketed after Herr Gutenberg's invention. And I totally agree with this choice.

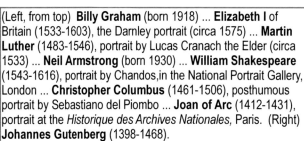

(Left, from top) **Billy Graham** (born 1918) ... **Elizabeth I** of Britain (1533-1603), the Darnley portrait (circa 1575) ... **Martin Luther** (1483-1546), portrait by Lucas Cranach the Elder (circa 1533) ... **Neil Armstrong** (born 1930) ... **William Shakespeare** (1543-1616), portrait by Chandos, in the National Portrait Gallery, London ... **Christopher Columbus** (1461-1506), posthumous portrait by Sebastiano del Piombo ... **Joan of Arc** (1412-1431), portrait at the *Historique des Archives Nationales,* Paris. (Right) **Johannes Gutenberg** (1398-1468).

Who Do You Like?

Think about the most influential writers you know (and you do not have to restrict yourself to the past thousand years). Personally, I would start with **Moses ben Amram** of the Tribe of Levi – the royally educated Hebrew in disguise as an Egyptian prince, who wrote the first five books of the Holy Bible. I would have to mention **David ben Jesse,** and his son **Solomon** – who gave us their poetry and wisdom in *Psalms* and *Proverbs.*

(Of course, I realize that David, trained only as a shepherd, was most likely illiterate, but certainly he had access to scholars and scribes who wrote down his words. I also accept that the Psalms and Proverbs were probably written by a variety of writers over a lengthy span of time – but the point is: David was a lyrical writer who expressed timeless, deep thoughts, and should be appreciated.)

I also include **Isaiah ben Amoz** of the Tribe of Judah and **Jeremiah ben Hilkiah** of the Tribe of Benjamin ... and I must acknowledge **Luke** of Antioch, **John ben Zebedee** and **Paul (Saul of Tarsus)** – writers of the New Testament. Where would we be without the Bible, that most significant Book of all books? **God** Himself is an Author!

Turning to two thousand years of *"after Christ"* (*anno domini:* "after the Christ") history, I choose **St. Augustine** (AD 354-430) ... **William Shakespeare** (1564-1616), of whose many excellent works I have memorized great portions ... **Samuel Langhorn "Mark Twain" Clemens** (1835-1910) ... **Clive Staples Lewis** (1898-1963) ... **John Ronald Reuel Tolkien** (1892-1973) ... and **Charles Monroe "Sparky" Schulz** (1923-2000).

"Wait a minute! In this illustrious list of great writers, you are including the cartoonist, Charles Schulz?" you may ask. Certainly! Great writers are not restricted to hardcover books – great writing can be found in a

(From top)
Moses (1391-1271 BCE), painting by Rembrandt ... **David** (1040-970 BC), sculpture by Michelangelo, Florence ... **Isaiah** (circa 800 BC), painting by Michelangelo, Sistine Chapel, Rome ... **Samuel L. "Mark Twain" Clemens** (1835-1910, photo by A.F. Bradley (1907) ... **Charles Monroe Schulz** (1923-2000).

cartoon's dialogue balloon. I have fiction writers as my favorites also: **Cecilia Holland** (born 1943), an excellent American novelist, who wrote my all-time favorite novel (which I re-read at least once a year), *Great Maria* ... and **Lady Dorothy Dunnett** (1923 - 2001), a marvelous historical writer from Scotland. These people bring much pleasure to my world of Reading, and their writing abilities continually inspire mine.

The first thing about being a good writer is to know whose writing you like ... and then to analyze **why** their writing appeals to you. It is likely you will unconsciously emulate your favorite writer's style ... which is **usually** a compliment.

What you read can have a lifelong impact on you. Learn what appeals, and why ... and be committed to your literary tastes. At the same time, do not be afraid to innovate, improvise, be creative – remembering: ***what you write may also have a lifelong impact on others.***

Moses finished speaking all these words to all Israel, and he said to them, "Set your hearts on all the words which I testify among you today, which you shall command your children to be careful to observe – all the words of this law. For it is not a futile thing for you, because it is your life, and by this word you shall prolong your days in the land which you cross over the Jordan to possess."

Deuteronomy 32:45-57

> What you read can have a lifelong impact on you.
> What you write may also have a lifelong impact on others.

"Most assuredly I say to you, he who heard My Word and believes in Him Who sent Me, has everlasting life, and shall not come into judgment but has passed from death into life. ... For if you believe Moses, you would

believe Me, for he wrote about Me. But if you do not believe his writings, how will you believe My words?"

Jesus Christ, cited in John 5:24, 46-47

There are **our** words written on the page ... and then there are **God's** words, which He inspires us to write:

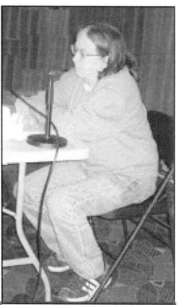

(Above) Author **Cecilia Holland** (born 1943)

(Below) *Great Maria*; published 1974

My son, do not forget My law, but let your heart keep My commands; for length of days and long life and peace they will add to you. Let not mercy and truth forsake you; bind them around your neck, write them on the tablet of your heart, and so find favor and high esteem in the sight of God and Man. ... My son, keep My words, and treasure My commands with you. Keep My commands and live, and My law as the apple of your eye. Bind them on your fingers, write them on the tablet of your heart.

Proverbs 3:1-4, 7:1-3

The Words of an Experienced Writer

I mentioned my all-time favorite novel is called *"Great Maria,"* written by American author **Cecilia Holland.** Ms. Holland has published 32 novels or more, and continues to publish regularly. Here is an excerpt from her autobiography:

I have been writing since I was 12. I told stories before then, to anybody who would listen, but in the summer after I turned 12, I

began having trouble keeping all the stories straight and decided to start writing them down. Since then, I've spent a good deal of every day writing.

I wrote historical fiction because, being 12, I had precious few stories of my own. History seemed to me then – as it still does – an endless fund of material. I liked novels because they were long and wide and deep. Every once in a great while, I try to write a poem, and now and then I write a short story, but I prefer novels.

When I was in college, I took a Creative Writing Course, *mostly to get a sure A. I wrote several little college girl stories for the teacher, poet* **William Meredith,** *until he said, "Enough already, what are you really interested in?" And I showed him the beginning of the novel I was trying to write. He liked that a lot; and when he left at the end of the semester, the next teacher, short-story writer* **David Jackson,** *liked it also, and they encouraged me to finish it. David took it to an editor-friend of his at* Atheneum. *They published it as* The Firedrake *in 1966. I had just dropped out of graduate school at* Columbia *to go work at* Bretano's *bookstore in midtown Manhattan, for $53 a week.*

Since then, I have written a lot, read a lot, raised my three wonderful daughters. I live in northern California, in the country. Once a week, I teach Creative Writing *at Pelican Bay State Prison, two hours away in Crescent City; and every day, I take care of a small menagerie of little animals.*

> I have known too many writers who have been "pregnant" with their books for years, even decades!

The keys I personally got from Cecilia's modest bio?

1. **She writes every day.**
2. **She has a great imagination,** and has learned to take "cold history facts" and uniquely breath life into personalities and events.
3. **She enjoys tackling large projects** ("*I liked novels because they were long and*

wide and deep"). In other words, she is not daunted by the task, does not give up easily, and aims toward the finish-line.

4.   **She networks with other writers,** and uses those connections to improve her own work. **Writing requires accountability.**

These are all principles which you will learn in greater detail in this book.

The Birth Experience

With every single writing project I have undertaken in my career as a professional writer, I have always felt like I was gestating and then giving birth. My husband and I have two wonderful, natural-born children, Jennifer and Alexander, and I thoroughly enjoyed both pregnancies and deliveries (and the ensuing years of parenthood). We probably should have had more children ... but the writing process for me has been my other expression of the ultimate act of creativity: **giving birth.**

Each writing project – whether all the individual components of a monthly magazine ... or a full-length book manuscript ... or even a comedy play written for performance in church – has the exact same steps:

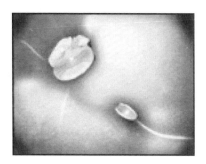

- **Conception**
- **Gestation**
- **Birth**
- **Child-rearing.**

Conception is when we get a little idea about something we want to write. I liken this to the creative union of sperm and ovum. In my opinion, life begins at conception – that is when God creates a human spirit and inserts it into that tiny burst of cells. When we begin a writing project, we do not fully know what it may become, but that joyful anticipation is part of the process.

Gestation is the **work** of writing. I have known too many writers who have been "pregnant" with a book for years, even decades! If only we will consider the gestation of a writing project to have a finite conclusion – such as a human pregnancy is known to have a 40-week duration – we will become very prolific as writers. Very few great writers are "one-hit wonders," and they cannot become greatly productive if they take half their lifetime to spit out one little book.

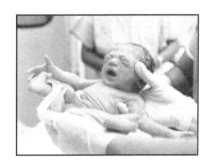 Just as expectant mothers will confer with other mothers, or first-time parents will take childbirth classes with other expectant parents, so it is that writers need to talk with other writers, to share their writing experiences, to learn helpful information and glean necessary encouragement to complete their own projects.

Delivery of our writing project can be very difficult. It takes hard work, dedication, perseverance, encouragement, to get the finished

 project from our word-processors or beyond our handwritten notepads, and launched out into the world. On a practical side, I believe it takes as long to work out a publication deal for a writing project as it does to actually write the project itself – I don't have any hard statistics to prove this, but it has certainly been my own experience.

Child-rearing (which also involves that nasty word "marketing") is the reward of watching our writing go out and impact the world. This is a tremendous joy, not in terms of ego or self-gratification but when we witness how the reader's life is impacted, changed, improved, enthused, clarified, enjoyed – all because they read what we write! Believing that Holy Spirit is watching every word we write, is pouring divine ideas into our brains, is working alongside us each stage of our writing – this is the difference between secular writing and Christian writing.

I will continually refer to these steps for successful writing. Some of my "kids" have been full-term but stillborn ... others have grown up and had offspring of their own. Some have given heartache (and maybe heartburn) ... others have brought tears of joyful fulfillment, especially when I have learned someone's heart was touched and turned toward Jesus Christ as a result of reading what I wrote. Just as the Spirit of God breathes life into that united conception of human sperm and ovum, so I believe He breathes life into the books we write for His glory.

Long after I am gone, I believe I will have left a legacy of Christ-honoring books for others to read. Who can say that Luke the Physician knew he was leaving a treasury for millions to read in the centuries that followed his life? Did **St. Francis of Assisi** know people would take his simple prayers and put them to music, singing them many hundreds of years later? We write because we love to write ... and because the Spirit enables us to do so. We carry on **His** legacy – for He was the first Writer/Creator.

In the beginning was THE WORD, and THE WORD was with God, and THE WORD was God.

John 1:1

Let the WORDS OF GOD shine through your writing!

- Why Is English So Hard To Learn?
- The bandage was wound around the wound.
- The farm was used to produce produce.
- The dump was so full that it had to refuse more refuse.
- We must polish the Polish furniture.
- He could lead if he would get the lead out.
- The soldier decided to desert his dessert in the desert.
- Since there is no time like the present, he thought it was time to present the present.
- When shot at, the dove dove into the bushes.
- I do not object to the object.
- The insurance was invalid for the invalid.
- There was a row among the oarsmen about how to row.
- They were too close to the door to close it.
- The wind was too strong to wind the sail.

Lesson One

(1) In your estimation, who are the three most influential people in the world of the past 100 years, and why?

_____

_____

_____

(2) Name your three favorite authors (historic or contemporary), and explain why you admire their work.

_____

_____

_____

(3) Why do **you** want to be a writer?

_____

_____

_____

(4) What is the most significant thing you got from this chapter?

_____

_____

_____

Chapter Two: *The Power and Permanence of* WORDS

As Christian writers, we recognize the gift of writing comes from the Supreme Author of all, therefore much of the training in this book will reflect our debt to Him:

In the beginning was the Word, and the Word was with God, and the Word was God.

John 1:1

From the beginning of Time, before writing was invented, people kept track of Life, their history, through the oral folklore of the story-tellers – those with vast memories and talents to recount the details accurately, and entertainingly. As various civilizations rose and fell, those civilizations who initially developed writing skills tended to endure past those who failed to record their history. It is not strange, then, that the ancient Egyptians – who continue to baffle scientists today with their inexplicable treasures of knowledge – were first among those who developed literature and created enduring ways to promote and store the written word. Therefore **Moses** – secret Hebrew turned Egyptian prince – was well-educated in the Egyptian manner ... which was obviously God's design because He had a later plan for His servant: to **write** the history of His people, as well as to **write down** the Laws which He gave them:

God is the One Who gifts us with writing. It is never just for our own enjoyment; our writing is often intended to change lives, possibly change nations. When God gives a person writing ability, we may not always see His purposes. But when we offer our talents back to Him, He works alongside us for His purposes.

And Moses turned and went down from the mountain, and the two tablets of the Testimony were in his hand. The tablets were written on both sides; on the one side and on the other they were written. Now the tablets were the work of God, and the writing was the writing of God on the tablets.

Exodus 32:15-17

Those Ten Commandments are still in force today these many millennia later. God was a great Writer ... and Moses was a pretty good scribe.

Rev. E.W. Kenyon (1867-1948)

What we write has a **tremendous** effect on people's lives. My memory from early childhood was riding endless hours in the back-seat of our 1956 Buick, since my father was an itinerant evangelist who traveled a great deal, and I recall hearing my mother reading aloud from the many wonderful writings of **Dr. E.W. Kenyon** – a man who died several years **before** I was born, yet who had a huge impact on my parents' ministry. Today Dr. Kenyon's writings are still revered and sought-after worldwide. My very understanding of the relationship of Heavenly Father with His Earthly children was strongly shaped by that man's prolific writings.

I believe that some day, what *I* write will have a tremendous effect on people's lives ... and I know that some day, what *you* will write will change the nations!

Your Word have I hidden in my heart that I might not sin against You.

Psalm 119:11

"For this is the covenant that I will make with the House of Israel after those days," says the Lord: *"I will put My laws in their mind and write them on their hearts, and I will be their God and they shall be My people."*

Hebrews 8:10

God Chooses Writers

Moses was educated to read and write. David used scribes to capture his words. Isaiah was a nobleman, likely well-educated. Luke was trained as a physician – despite that handicap, we can actually *read* his writing! Paul was educated in the rabbinical tradition.

God is the One Who gifts us with writing. It is never a gift just for our own enjoyment, for our writing is often intended to change lives, possibly change nations. When God gives a person writing ability, we may not always see His intent – but when we offer our talents back to Him, He works alongside us for His purpose. Where would we be today without the writings of these great men of God?

> ## What Makes A Writer?
>
> ❖ A writer loves to read!
> ❖ A writer has imagination
> ❖ The prophet Jeremiah wrote: "This fire is shut up in my bones, and I cannot restrain myself!" (Jeremiah 20:9).

Writers Love Words

I have never yet met a talented writer who was not also a voracious reader. And I have never known an exceptional writer who was not also a keen observer of the world around him ... especially other people. We can learn much from other writers ... and we can learn much from looking beyond the pages of a book to see the world itself. A good writer will be a truth-teller: **one who reports as accurately as possible what he sees and hears.** Reality will always ring true to your reader.

Widely-read people are better contestants in trivia contests and on game shows. For years my family urged me to try as a contestant on *Jeopardy!* because I would often calmly call out the answers before the on-air contestants did ... and I was usually correct. When *Who Wants to Be a Millionaire?* made its first big splash on TV, I generally tracked evenly with the progressively more difficult questions. Why? Because I love reading. I may have made a lot of money as a contestant because I have always loved to read, and reading has always been a great source of good general knowledge.

Above: Author **Harper Lee** (born 1926)

Below) *To Kill a Mockingbird*; published 1960

This was discovered when I was 8 years old. My precocity as a child was largely revealed because my Grade Three teacher "caught" me reading a novel, **Harper Lee's** brilliant *"To Kill a Mockingbird,"* which was then required-reading for Grade Ten students. My teacher asked me if I understood what I was reading; when I answered affirmatively, she quickly asked more questions to test my comprehension, knowledge and vocabulary. When those proved sound, they submitted me to a battery of extensive tests – and the outcome was determined that at age 8 I had an IQ of 163. It was then decided I should be advanced into the next grade – all because I loved to read!

The more you read, the better your grammar becomes, the quicker your spelling improves, the larger your vocabulary grows. Learning to love words – to understand them, to use them correctly, even to play with them (naturally I love working crossword puzzles and all sorts of word-based games) -- is essential to being a good writer. When in High School, I elected to take Latin by correspondence because I thought I would have a better grasp of **all** the Romantic languages – such as Italian, Spanish, German, English – which are all Latin-based ... and therefore I would be a better wordsmith. Today I own a Latin audio course which I dip into on occasion to refresh my memory. (NOTE: English is **not** the most logical, consistent language on Earth – especially illogical in spelling and grammar – but it is the most common; see sidebar on page 37.)

Writers are Communicators

Brother-in-law Ken Nyman with my sister Marisa.

My brother-in-law **Ken Nyman** is a quiet-spoken man. At our large, rollicking Tribe of Gossett activities, he is often "seen but not much heard" (that is, except when our family plays competitive games, then Ken can be very funny, outspoken and boisterous). Yet Ken is a person who expresses himself very well in writing – he quite coherently presents outstanding thoughts and unique viewpoints in his writing, whether his message is delivered by email or accompanies his signature on a greeting card. A good writer can express his deepest thoughts in writing – and realizes that what he writes will follow him as long as paper endures (or the Internet continues).

Which brings me to the point that writers can also make **mistakes.** A well-known Christian evangelist approached me several years ago, about to ask for help in writing his first autobiographical book. We never concluded those negotiations, and he subsequently contracted another ghostwriter to produce that first manuscript. When that book was initially published, it was discovered to contain substantial doctrinal errors – that is, the ghostwriter had included some of his own doctrinal beliefs which clashed with the evangelist's beliefs – and, very embarrassingly and expensively, the evangelist had to retract the entire book, offer public apologies and corrections of the misinformation, and have the whole manuscript rewritten and republished. The controversy around that first book was incendiary ... and perhaps the evangelist and I really should have completed our original negotiations.

The crux is: what you write (and publish) has endurance, for good or for ill. What Moses wrote those many thousands of years ago is still kicking around today. What Paul wrote two thousand years ago continues to impact our generation in today's world. What Shakespeare wrote four hundred years ago is still considered the most lyrical and insightful English ever written. What Dr. Kenyon wrote nearly one hundred years ago is still sending people to their Bibles to check it out today.

Education is not everything. As I previously said, David the Psalmist was most likely not a trained journalist or songwriter – in fact, he was probably illiterate – but he worked with "the Chief Musician" (and, no doubt, a full staff of scribes) to ensure that we have access to the beauty of his "conversations" with and about God. I have never maintained that a good writer must also be well-educated – in fact, I think dry, boring lectures on writing by dry, boring professors can produce (satirical drum-roll) dry, boring writers.

I believe a good writer loves to read anything and everything (thus becoming self-educated), and then learns to express his heart in his own words. When I went to college, for instance, my major study was Theatre, and my minor interest was Journalism. It was not until some years later that I was able to put my natural writing ability to work in such a way that it became my profession ... and my passion.

World-Wide Impact

Another aspect of the endurance of books is that they rarely stay silently on a dusty shelf, but have a unique tendency to travel around the world. I have accompanied my father on numerous overseas evangelistic trips, and **in every single country** I have visited (which is but a fraction of where Dad has ministered), I have seen his books precede his in-person ministry. Dad has five natural-born children, but hundreds – probably thousands – of people who call him their "spiritual father" because they first read his books. People who were plucked out of gutters, whose lives were changed completely, who saw tremendous healings, who established tremendous churches – all because one of Dad's almost 200 titles had made it into their hands first.

A young man named **Joseph Prince** – the child of a Buddhist and a Hindu, raised as an agnostic – saw one of my father's books, *There's Dynamite in Praise,* in the window of a psychic bookstore in Singapore. (How in the world did an outright Christian book get into an occult bookstore?) He read the title, thought, *"That sounds like a good book on spiritual power,"* went inside and bought the book, read it through twice ... and became a born-again Christian. He contacted my father and asked him to become his spiritual father and mentor ... and today Joseph pastors the largest Charismatic church in Singapore. Do you think it is remotely possible that our writings can be used in such a way? We do not know, but there **is** that possibility that when we send our little books out into the big, big world ... that lives will be changed!

Some of Dad's book show up at his public meetings looking very ragged and well-read – those are the most beautiful copies of all! Some have been translated (officially and unofficially) into dozens of languages; others have been photocopied, stapled together and distributed into underground churches in countries where Christianity is outlawed, or into villages where poverty prohibits the luxury of purchasing a book. God anointed my father to write those books ...

Top: **Joseph Prince** (born 1963).

Middle: ***There's Dynamite In Praise*** (first published 1974).

Bottom: **Don E. Gossett** (born 1929)

and their impact on the world will continue to be felt long after Dad goes on to his Heavenly Reward.

We can becomes writers just to please ourselves ... but we need to be aware that **our writing** can jump way past our reach – and change lives forever.

Lesson Two

(1) How would you edit and improve the following paragraph?

Julie Pruitt a Burch Bay resident is convinced you can teach old dogs new tricks. Pruit who is a volunteer foster parent for senior dogs has organized a benefit walk for dogs of all ages on Saturday 23 at Birch Bay State Park to raise money for Old Dog Haven a non-profit dog adoption agency in Arlington. "This is not just for old dogs walking. This is for any age dog walking in support of old dogs." she said.

_____

_____

_____

_____

(2) Write a simple four-line rhyme, just to practice using words.

_____

_____

_____

_____

(3) What is the most significant thing you learned in this chapter?

_____

_____

_____

Chapter Three: *Start With the End in Mind*

I always encourage people to write about what they **know.** It is true that some of my favorite authors (such as historical writers) write about events which took place hundreds of years ago, or events which *might* take place hundreds of years in the future (science-fiction writers). These people are fictional novelists – and I **love** their expressions in writing. But rarely do new writers succeed in total fiction – they are better equipped to start writing about what they know: real life.

Most of us have heard about or watched "reality TV." The fact that all of their camera-shots are totally pre-planned and staged, and everyone is wearing pinned-on microphones takes that out of genuine reality and puts it into entertainment. There is, however, such a thing as "reality writing," which is based on two principles: ***"Good writers are always truth-tellers"*** and ***"Reality always rings true with your readers."*** Especially with popular fiction, if your reader can't track with your book because the imaginary world you created is fuzzy or unbelievable, they won't continue reading past chapter 1 or 2.

The best fiction writers I know – Christian or otherwise – have started writing real-life stories and articles before they ventured into viable fiction. Part of her diagnostic treatment for clinical depression prompted Joanne K. Rowling, author of the mega-popular *"Harry Potter"* books, to begin writing out her own feelings; this cathartic exercise was amplified upon the tragic death of her mother from multiple sclerosis. Drawing on childhood memories and feelings of loss and grief, Ms. Rowling created a magical alternative to an unhappy life, pouring much of her own personality into her protagonist *Harry Potter*

> This chapter's title, "Start with the end in mind," is a favorite phrase of motivational speakers. It means exactly what it says: any successful writing project must be thought through right to the end before a single word is written down.

> Knowing where you are starting ... where you are going ... and where you are ending is essential to planning and executing any writing project.

(although there's a lot of her in *Hermione Granger* too). She said, *"From the very first page, I knew where Harry was going to go in the very last book. His adventure from childhood to adulthood was always pointed to that one finishing, defining moment. Harry was the hero that I wanted to become."* J.K. Rowling started the *Harry Potter* series with the end-goal firmly in mind ... and he grew up out of her own personal life.

The Running Story

My husband Kenneth is an avid runner. He does not look like a typical runner, who are generally lanky, long-limbed, bone-thin, hollow-faced ... whereas Kenneth is short and stocky – but he loves to run. For some reason truly unknown to me, for Christmas 1997, I gave him a few books written by and about famous runners, which were intended to encourage Kenneth in his quest for fitness and health. I did not realize I was unleashing a running machine!

After reading these books and some running magazines, he decided to aim for the world-famous Seattle Marathon, which was held in November that year of 1998. In January 1998, Kenneth began to train for the race. He subscribed to different monthly magazines devoted to running, and he simply devoured them (and left them in strategic places all over the house). He learned running tips and about nutrition plans, interval training and what kind of shoes to wear – all sorts of things that would help him succeed as a runner.

First, he ran five miles. Then he increased to 10-mile runs. He would drive to a specific point in the countryside and plant a bottle of water at the halfway point of his intended run, so he would be able to rehydrate himself. By late spring, he was logging 15 miles and more runs several times a week. He ran in local half-marathons, just for the experience. He became obsessed! I was very proud of him ... and sorry for myself because I have "detached" kneecaps (the result of a long-ago snow-skiing injury) which prohibit me from trying to keep up with him for more than a mile or two.

In October 1998, our son Alex returned from several months of overseas missionary work, and he decided he would join his father at the Seattle Marathon. This was quite unfair: Kenneth, at age 47, had been training for nearly a year ... and Alex, at age 20, trained (with his father) for only one month. But they both had this passion for running ... and that competitive Marathon loomed before them. Not that they thought the would ever **win** the race which attracted hundreds of skilled runners from around the world ... but just the thought of **completing** the 26.4-mile course would put them into a different category of human being: **demi-god!**

On a wet and windy day in late November, our daughter Jennifer, her young son Kristian, and I stood on the sideline at Mile 21 and waited for our heroes to come running by. We held changes of shirts for them and much loving encouragement to share with them. Shortly after they passed on – just he and Alex reached Mile 24 – Kenneth pulled a muscle in his left leg ... so while Jen, Kristian and I waited (impatiently) in the grandstand at the Seattle Center Stadium, where the Marathon was concluding, we did not know that Alex had thoughtfully slowed his pace to stay with his injured father. They finally completed their 26.4-mile race in ... well, okay, it was not a great time – in fact, they were chagrined to be bested by a 72-year-old man – but they entered the stadium to the cheers of hundreds of well-wishers. I treasure the photograph of them limping together down that last hundred yards. They had

Kenneth and Alex Halsey reach the finish line of the Seattle Marathon. (1998)

completed a Marathon!

How like **Hebrews 12:1**:

Therefore we also, since we are surrounded by so great a cloud of witnesses, let us lay aside every weight and the sin which so easily ensnares us, and let us run with endurance the race that is set before us.

This is when I shared an idea with Kenneth: "Honey, let's write a book together about 'running the race.' You could bring all your experience as a Marathon runner – from your training, through trials, through enduring the actual race even with injuries – and I could parallel it with Biblical teaching of living out our Christian lives." That book is simply titled *Running the Race*. The reason I shared this lengthy story is: I always believe it is important to write honestly about what you know ... and creatively present it so it will have an impact on others, most often pointing them toward Jesus Christ.

WARNING!

It is always advisable to b a l a n c e writing passion with real life. N e v e r f a l l prey to loving w r i t i n g s o much that you are a "human doing" instead of a "human being."

Write about what you know. Do you already write in any of these genres?

✳ Songs
✳ Fiction
✳ Non-Fiction
✳ Articles
✳ Essays
✳ Speeches
✳ Advertising
✳ Correspondence
✳ Journals

The truth is that creative writers should be willing to write in **all** these genres, at different times of their careers.

The Writer's Tree

When I undertake a book project, I always start with the skeleton of the material. I determine if I am dealing with "a small child" or "a large adult" (and in the case of one particular project, I felt like I had birthed twins or triplets). Knowing where you are starting ... where you are going ... and where you are ending – this is essential to planning and executing any writing project.

First, ask yourself, *"What are the elements of a tree?"* Every tree is the same: it began with a seed ... it put down roots ... it grew up a trunk ... the trunk spread into branches ... the branches sprouted limbs and shoots ... the limbs sprouted buds ... the buds became leaves and flowers and fruit.

The **seed** of your writing is **the single idea, the dream.** In J.K. Rowling's case, she wanted to re-imagine her own life, dealing with sadness and loss, yet still come out the winner. Often an idea is simply a concept; the journey of fleshing it out and making it real on paper is what writing is all about.

Once the seed is planted and is given life, the first thing it does is **put down roots.** Roots are the **theme** or the **outline.** Without this stable foundation, your writing will falter ... and possibly topple over before it is done. Why? Because it **is** surprisingly easy to forget **why** we are writing something. This is **not** "creativity overflowing" – it is losing focus. The roots are knowing **why** you are writing.

The next step is the **trunk,** which is the strength of your writing project, the **what** you are writing about. This element will carry your project from its beginning to its end, drawing up nutrition from beneath the soil (the roots) and soaring your writing into the sky. This is **planning** and **executing** the project, also known as **research.** Knowing about **what** you are writing is doing your homework before you get started.

The **branches** are the chapters – or in an article, the paragraphs. The characteristics of the chapters have already been determined by the roots and the trunk; this is **how** the project is written. A novel by Frank Peretti will have enough chapters – and his chapters are surprisingly short – to keep the reader interested and moving through the story. A novel by Arthur Haley, however, might have such a broad range that he actually writes mini-books within the major book. For that he first does massive research which holds together all the elements; thus, his books require a very deep root system and a very strong trunk. The research often suggests the branches.

Continuing with the Tree Analogy, the next step is the **limbs,** which is the **content,** the actual narrative. When I write, I tend to think in whole sentences, then in paragraphs. That is, having planned what I want to say in a chapter, I often start by jotting the subtitles first, then fleshing in the content. Making notes or using subtitles is a habit I highly recommend because it helps keep you from getting lost going on proverbial rabbit trails.

The final component of the Tree consists of the **leaves, the flowers, the fruit.** This means the **words** you use, the vocabulary you express as you write, the **colors** you literally paint. Your *first draft* may not be very colorful or dynamic, but as you re-read, you may realize: *"Hmm, I should have used 'majestic' instead of 'good-looking' or 'blood-thirsty' instead of 'bad.'"* Even if you don't have a goal to win a Pulitzer Prize, the "foliage" of your tree needs to be outstanding!

If you will keep the Writer's Tree concept tucked in your mind as you write any project, I guarantee you will make it from beginning to end.

Trade Secrets

There are several rules to follow when building your framework, and I'll give them to you one-by-one.

Pick a beginning
... a middle ...
and an ending for your book

Someone who considers writing his life story will say, *"But I have not died yet, so I do not know how far to take this book."* True, so respond, *"Decide somewhere you will finish **this** book – maybe five years or so before this current date – and then, if you want, you can write a sequel, which picks up at the point where you finish this book."* In 2007, I implored my good friend Larry Norman, a noted Christian songwriter, to let me help him write his autobiography; he hesitated ... and he died in 2009, with no authorized legacy (but many barracudas who jumped in and wrote their own redoubtable versions of Larry's colorful life).

Many are aware that honored author J.R.R. Tolkein wrote the wonderful *"The Lord of the Rings"* Trilogy as **one long book,** but the publisher decided to maximize their marketing opportunities and broke it up into three separate yet connected books: *"The Fellowship of the*

Ring" ... "The Two Towers" ... "The Return of the King." Makes sense, doesn't it?

Most would-be writers get intimidated by the scope of a project and decide, *"This is just too big for me to tackle!"* – and they are probably correct. So learn to chop up a topic into smaller chunks and write them one stage at a time. This is the same as the old joke: *"How do you eat an elephant? One bite at a time!"*

Perhaps consider it this way: if you are going to learn to play the piano, you do not start out with sheet music for a beautiful concerto – you start out with *A-B-C-D-E-F-G.* You begin by learning to play scales ... so why would you think a novice writer is going to begin with a 2,000-page novel? Start simply, and the flow of your work – from beginning, to middle, to end – will come.

The next "trade secret" is one I stumbled on by myself, only to learn later it is commonly used by editors – but not so much by rookie writers! Most editors wish their writing staff would work as methodically as this because it would make their work more professional and bring it in on time. *"What's the secret?"* you ask.

The absolutely most important thing you will ever write for your manuscript is the
Table of Contents (or Outline)

A Table of Contents is like a road-map that will take you from the beginning, all the way through the middle, and to the end. Consulting with your Table of Contents from time to time throughout the initial writing stage is like one of those maps in shopping malls with "You Are Here" in big letters on a red arrow. That is why, when I begin a writing project, I write out the Table of Contents, print it and stick it up nearby in my office, so it catches my eye. Even if a Table of Contents undergoes changes, it still functions like a road-map or an architect's plans.

Another way to look at this is using the analogy of baking a **Chocolate Cake.** You can pull out your favorite recipe from the recipe card file, assemble all the ingredients, start to measure and blend and stir ... and then realize that you forgot that one little ingredient called: chocolate! If you forget to add chocolate to your Chocolate Cake, you will end up with a Vanilla Cake. Establishing the Table of Contents first is like having the right recipe and then following the directions; it helps you identify items you  may be lacking or have overlooked in your research. I believe that frequently consulting the Table of Contents can single-handedly keep a writing project from going astray.

The last "trade secret" here is one that few people want to talk about, and rarely want to adhere to, but one of which I cannot stress enough its importance:

Establish incremental deadlines

Creating realistic deadlines enables the writer to maintain them. Some people, like me, work well under deadline pressure, but that is not typical or optimally recommended. Incremental deadlines are important to keep a project on time, to help each stage proceed as efficiently as possible, and to actually **reach** that last step successfully. When you are writing for someone else, a thorough and honest discussion of each person's deadline responsibilities is essential and **must** be taken seriously.

This concept really came home to me when I undertook the job as Managing Editor of a monthly print magazine. Gone were the days when I could twiddle here and twiddle there on a full-length book project, taking six months or ten months or two years to complete the manuscript. Now I had to hone my skills to:

(1) Pick the major theme for each magazine issue (although we generally chose themes on an annual basis);

(2) Consult with my superiors about their preferences for the next issue;

(3) Lay out the "blank book" (deciding how many pages we would publish, based on how much paid advertising we anticipated);

(4) Decide the articles that best suited each theme, and assign them to the writers;

(5) Determine what photographic support and/or graphic artwork would be needed for each article, and book the photographers' schedule and notify the Art Department of our requirements;

(6) Manage input from my creative staff (having already given them specific deadlines like, "I need this article finished by October 10th");

(7) Schedule the Printing House for their production run (this date could vary sometimes if we were printing a larger edition) and then being sure our basic material was delivered to them in advance or at least on time;

(8) Notify the Mailing Department to run our address labels by a certain date;

(9) Have all the support materials (page masters, photographs, artwork) included with the final layout of the magazine safely delivered to the Printing House;

(10) Be sure the finished magazines were returned to the Mailing Department for their participation (attaching labels, bundling magazines, delivery to the post office, etc.), and appropriate mailings took place.

We did all these stages every 30 days – and then started over again, month after month! There was no room for missing deadlines, no clean-ups of missed materials. I admit that when I first started the job, my staff and I pulled more than a few all-nighters, but as I improved at my job, I became "religious" about those incremental deadlines. In later years, no longer working on a monthly magazine, I found that adherence to incremental deadlines made me more

> I love deadlines.
> I especially like
> the whooshing
> sound they make
> as they fly by.

productive.

Conversely, working with clients who never understood or conformed to incremental deadlines also became a major headache for me. What part of *"Read through this First Draft; make notes about what parts you want to change; get the First Draft back to me within 30 days"* did they not understand? When I am juggling several projects at once, having one fall off the calendar is nearly disastrous! *"What do you mean?"*

Let's use "Book A" and "Book B" as examples; you are the Writer/Editor and your client is the Author. The First Draft of Book A is written and sent to Author A on January 31st. Author A has until March 1st to read through, notate changes (sometimes consulting by phone), and get it back to you. In the meantime, you are working on Book B, and the First Draft of Book B duly goes to its Author on March 1st and is expected to be returned by April 30th. In the meantime, Author A has not returned Book A's First Draft by March 1st, so you raise your eyebrows but continue with other writing projects. Then Author B returns Book B's First Draft on April 20th (*"Well done!"*), hoping you will be able to address his changes right away because he knows that the Final Draft is scheduled for May 31st.

Then Author A returns the First Draft of Book A on June 1st, three months past the deadline. And he wants to get his book published in time for a major book fair in July, meaning he needs hard copies in his hands by June 15th. Does he expect you to drop Book B's timeline just because he did not adhere to the reasonable incremental deadline you had both agreed to? Who is at fault? Well, I suppose the argument could be made that you failed to sufficiently impress upon Author A the **severe importance of incremental deadlines.** Unfortunately, my experience has been that few Authors truly understand what standards a professional Writer must adhere to, having significant tunnel vision about their own needs, so give yourself a break.

Even when you are simply writing your own projects, maintaining incremental deadlines – *"Finish research by January 31st ... finish first draft by July 1st ... finish rewrite by October 1st"* – makes you a better, quicker, **more intentional** writer. Many writers never get past the First Draft stage because they don't realize that a **First Draft is merely one step in the process** and not the perfect Final product. They get drowned in tweaking one paragraph over and over, never realizing that they need to push on through the Table of Contents, adhering to Incremental Deadlines.

This may make more sense if you ever ask someone to analyze your manuscript. You turn your precious baby over to someone else's reading, and then you wait anxiously to hear their response. You wait ... and you wait ... and you wonder, and have second-thoughts about that fourth paragraph of chapter six ... and you wait, and you wait. Instead of putting yourself through all that agony, say this: *"Would you read this through and get it back to me by tomorrow" or "... this Friday?"* It is imperative that you **never** allow anyone else's critique of your work slow you down so much that you lose momentum. **You** know what your Final Deadline is, but if you miss deadlines because of someone else's tardiness, your Editor won't be unhappy with **them!**

There is nothing wrong with tweaking – it is, in fact, a common habit of good writers – but as your writing skills improve, you will likely discover you just know that a little change here or there will make your project that much better. Personally, I have invariably remembered something I wished I had changed just after I have couriered the Final Draft manuscript to the publisher! Tweaking is okay if you do not miss your actual incremental deadlines.

Treat deadlines seriously. When you are working for someone else – such as a client or a publisher – your deadlines are very real and meaningful to them as well.

"Start with the end in mind" means that you know what you want your manuscript to accomplish. Is it a children's book – will there be illustrations? Is it aimed at an unsaved audience – and are you willing to take harsh criticism? Rarely do books that were conceived as "just my ramblings" make it into publication. Organize your thoughts, your tools, your talents ... and bring your best effort to every single writing project you undertake.

Lesson Three

(1) In a very simple manner, relate a single true incident from your own life, in a way that would have appeal (relate to) a 6-year-old child:

_____

_____

_____

(2) Now write that same incident as if you were reporting it in *USAToday:*

_____

_____

_____

(3) What is the single most important thing you learned from this chapter – and why and how are you going to use it in your own writing?

_____

_____

_____

Chapter Four: *Target Your Audience*

Never try to write a book for absolutely everyone in the whole world. Despite what the Apostle Paul wrote – *"Just as I also please men in all things"* (1 Corinthians 10:33) – we **cannot** be *"all things to all men"* with our writing and genuinely be successful. We cannot write a book for the young American who likes Rap music ... and still expect it to perfectly cross the cultures to an unsophisticated grandmother living in a Third World country. We cannot roll out multi-syllable words, and expect it will make sense to a person who has little or no education. We would not expect a four-year-old child to understand *"Brain Surgery in Six Easy Lessons"* (and I advisedly use that analogy because in September 2006, I did have brain surgery!).

Professor Phil

I have a wonderful brother-in-law, **Phillip Howard Wiebe, PhD,** who is formerly Chair of the Department of Philosophy, Professor of Philosophy and former Dean of Arts and Religious Studies at Trinity Western University in Langley, British Columbia, Canada (that's the way Wikipedia writes it). Phillip is a brilliant man, top in his profession, and well-respected among his peers and students. He is the author of several books – writing and publishing papers and manuscripts is required for his ongoing professorship – and I deeply admire him. He also usually wins at *Skip-Bo™* after one of our extended family dinner parties (smile).

Above: Dr. Phillip H. Wiebe

Below: "Visions of Jesus"

As Phil was writing one of his books, *"Visions of Jesus,"* I tracked with him as he went through years and years of research, querying him about his journeys around the world to interview people who told amazing

true stories about seeing or experiencing a physical presence of Christ Jesus in their lives. When that particular book was published, to much acclaim, I eagerly read his final product ... and in all honesty, as much we had already discussed the topic, I could hardly follow the book itself. It was written in such a scholarly manner, with thorough academic arguments for and against the concept of physical manifestations, but despite my own intelligence, I admit I got lost in the book. Phillip intentionally targeted his book for the academic world – but I personally did not complete my second year of college. His target audience was his professional peers, not the average middle-class consumer. Phillip makes no apology for that because **he targeted his audience** and hit the mark accurately.

A classic mistake first-time writers make is trying to address too many people with their burning message, usually producing a vague product. I always **visualize** the people to whom I am writing:

Top: Our daughter-in-law Cherry Halsey, with Jude, Aja and Hayley

Second: Jeanne with Laurel Rudolph

Third: Mystery man (identity concealed)

Bottom: Anne Ryan and her granddaughter Audrey Ryan, and Jeanne

• if it's a children's book, I imagine reading it with my grandchildren **Jude, Aja and Hayley** (our son Alex's young children);
• if I'm writing a fund-raising letter, I picture **Laurel Rudolph** (a beloved long-time friend) responding to the appeal;
• if I'm writing a magazine article about the advantages of Christianity, I try to perceive it the way **Peter and Doreen** (some non-Christian friends) might absorb it – and this is admittedly one of the more difficult applications for me since I have been a Christian my entire life;
• if I'm writing a comedy skit for presentation at church, I project how **Anne Ryan** (our pastor's wife and one of my closet friends) is going to react.

I would not verbiage in the children's story that I would use in the fund-raising project, and vice versa – which would be counter-productive to both audiences. As President Abraham Lincoln said: *"You can please some of the people some of the time, but you cannot please all of the people all of the time."* And we must remember: we cannot know where our writing will go or who will be reading it at any given time.

Popular Christian authors Jerry B. Jenkins and Tim LaHaye – whose acclaimed *"Left Behind"* series has been successfully translated into cinema – also re-wrote their series to capture a totally different target audience: children and young people. They realized that the same story needed to be told a little differently for a younger audience, which was smart and market-savvy.

Sarah, Reinhard and Paul

As I am involved in a writing project, I continually endeavor to remind myself: *"Would this paragraph make sense to my target audience?"* Sometimes I have deleted (more on "deletions" later) entire chapters, realizing I had lost sight of my audience while the work was in progress. We can become so involved in expressing ourselves that we can forget someone else is going to read this. This principle is especially important for me as a ghost-writer, because my clients have many different audiences and I must focus on them very clearly and carefully.

Years ago I wrote two books for Sarah Bowling, *"Solutions"* and *"Fearless On the Edge,"* who has a tremendous ministry especially to young people. Her books were breezy and conversational, filled with colloquialisms and humor – and I'm thankful to say the finished products ended up **sounding just like her,** and successfully addressed her target audience.

Immediately following these two books was a huge

Top: Sarah Bowling

Middle: Reinhard Bonnke

Bottom: Paul Overstreet

project for Reinhard Bonnke, who has a massively effective international ministry as an evangelist, with particular emphasis on soul-winning. His book, *"Mark My Words,"* was more somber and intense, hard-hitting and precise – and again I believe I captured his German personality accurately and that I concisely targeted his international audience.

Right on the heels of Reinhard's lengthy project was a book written for a down-home country boy, Paul Overstreet, who is an acclaimed writer and singer of Country music. Paul has a Nashville drawl and those natural Southern manners, and his song-fans love his music. Production of this book, *"Forever and Ever, Amen,"* was highlighted for me by an afternoon phone call by the person Paul had asked to write the Foreword: I was surprised and delighted to receive a phone call from Randy Travis, the Country singer who won awards for his rendition of the song *"Forever and Ever, Amen."* By the end of this book, I think my Oklahoma-born drawl had been resurrected in my daily conversation.

I do not think casual Sarah's typical audience would get as much out of the very-Teutonic Reinhard's book as they would enjoy Sarah's all-American books, and vice versa. It is possible Sarah's readers and

Paul's readers may have more in common. Different audiences, different personalities, different approaches.

It is also possible I was somewhat schizophrenic by the time I completed Paul's project ... sigh for my poor family! As a ghost-writer I had used my God-given talents to speak with three different voices to three different audiences in three different projects. Staying focused on your specific audience will help you keep the project moving along in the right direction.

Alex and SBS

This principle is also illustrated by **Inductive Bible Study** (IBS). Several time I have done wonderful inductive Bible studies in my private devotions and with study groups, and I understand and practice the basic forms of that kind of study. However, our son Alexander took IBS to a new level when he taught the **School of Biblical Studies** (SBS), which is one of the hundreds of wonderful classes offered by *Youth With A Mission* (YWAM) to its thousands of students around the world.

Alex teaching the School of Biblical Studies at the YWAM University of the Nations in Lonavala, Maharashtra, India (2005)

It began when Alex complained in the kindest possible way to Kenneth and me. *"Mom, Dad, you did a pretty good job of teaching Jen and me as children about God, about the Bible, about Christianity. But as an adult, I realized I simply didn't know enough about the Bible itself, so I am going to learn it, read it, study it, and become proficient in it."* Alex was in his early 20s at this stage, and already had several years of serving with YWAM; the SBS was only available after he had done YWAM "boot camp" called **Discipleship Training School** (DTS). [Every single school conducted in YWAM follows the same basic principle: the lecture phase, followed immediately by the outreach phase; what the student learns in the lecture phase must be put to use in the outreach phase.]

One of the unique features of the SBS is that every student not only **reads** the entire Bible through **at least five times** during the 9-month school, but they also **write** it out, sometimes paraphrasing, sometimes making it applicable to their own circumstances (Alex mostly wrote his on his laptop computer because his personal handwriting is somewhat atrocious). Alex began his SBS studies in Turner Valley, Alberta, Canada, then completed the course in England; his outreach phase was in India. Then Alex joined the YWAM Base in Budapest, Hungary, where he led DTS schools for several years. Then he switched to teaching the SBS course in Budapest, and later in India.

The next step in Alex's international schooling and teaching career eventually led him to establish a YWAM Base in Ranchi, Jharkhand, a northern province of India. Oh, and he also got married to a beautiful Indian girl, Cherry Ruth Beck – and they started a family, which now

A graduating class of the Biblical Academy at the Life-Giving Network Base in Ranchi, Jharkhand, India. Alex and his wife Cherry are at the far left. (2011)

includes a son, Jude, and two daughters, Aja and Hayley. Eventually the SBS taught at the Ranchi YWAM Base morphed into the **Biblical Academy** as a division of the **Life-Giving Network** sponsored by our home church; this is a church-planting initiative which enables Alex and his fellow teachers instruct fledgling pastors and missionaries, equipping them for church-planting in their own cities, villages and slum ministries.

But getting back to the SBS and Alex's own experience: a critical part of the SBS is realizing that the Bible was written **for the people of that day;** this is called **The Original Reader** (TOR) concept. SBS students, applying the TOR concept, would fully understand the following somewhat cryptic passage:

Now on the first day of Unleavened Bread, when they killed the Passover lamb, His disciples said to Him, "Where do You want us to go and prepare, that You may eat the Passover?"

And He sent two of His disciples and said to them, "Go into the city, and a man will meet you carrying a pitcher of water; follow him. Wherever he goes in, say to the master of the house, 'The Teacher says: Where is the guest room in which I may eat the Passover with My disciples?' Then he will show you a large upper room, furnished and prepared; there make ready for us."

So His disciples went out, and came into the city and found it just as He said to them; and they prepared the Passover.

Mark 14:12-16

"What is cryptic about that?" We must understand that in Jesus' First Century era, a water carrier was usually either a slave or a woman – rarely a (free) man. It is my belief that an active "underground church" was in formation during the years of Jesus' ministry, and this clandestine group continued well after His death, resurrection and ascension. We know that Jesus' teachings were not popular with the Jewish religious leaders ... therefore I believe His followers realized they were going to have to behave circumspectly in public to prevent harassment by the authorities.

Thus, when Jesus instructed His disciples to *"look for a **man** carrying a pitcher of water,"* He was clueing them into a "secret sign" of how to find a "safe house" where they could meet quietly and in safety. Remember: this was just before His arrest by the San Hedrin – and they didn't arrest Him at this "safe house" but waited until Judas Iscariot tipped them off to His presence in an unguarded place, the Garden of Gethsemane.

That's a lengthy explanation to illustrate this point: what may be obscure to use and easily overlooked was, in fact, a clear flag to TOR of the book of Mark. Mark knew who his target audience would be ... and it was **not** the people of the 21st Century, who get their water on demand by way of a copper pipe running into their insulated houses and pouring either hot or cold from a faucet.

Although we may be illustrating timeless

spiritual principles, we should never expect that First Century and Twenty-First Century readers automatically make sense to each other. If you wrote:

How well God must like you – you don't hang out at Sin Saloon, you don't slink along Dead-End Road, you don't go to Smart-Mouth College!

– would that vernacular make sense to the people of the Psalmist-King David's time? No, he wrote it this way:

Blessed is the man who walks not in the counsel of the ungodly, nor stands in the way of sinners, nor sits in the seat of the scornful.

That's **Psalm 1:1,** first in *The Message,* then in the *New King James* version.

In *"The Message,"* the brilliant Eugene H. Peterson translated Psalm 1:1 from David's writings nearly 3,000 years ago so that we can read it richly today. Dr. Peterson understood the target audience of David's day, yet he brought the same timeless truth into our speech and thought ... much the same as Mr. Jenkins and Dr. LaHaye did when they re-wrote their last-days prophetic series for a younger audience.

[Note: it was because I had studied and learned about TOR, the life and times of Biblical people (such as the example of the free male water-carrier) that I was inspired to write *"That Which I Ought To Do,"* which is a novel loosely based on the life of the Apostle Paul. I created fictional characters -- such as "Sarah," the wife of Stephen (the boyhood friend of Saul of Tarsus, later the first Christian martyr) – and wove a story about forgiveness and restoration. Research is a **great** thing to do ... and we never know what dividends it could pay.]

Not having a specific audience in mind can also have cross-cultural complications. I wrote a book for a pastor from California who related an incident which took place in his childhood. Carl had a younger brother Brian, and the two little boys decided to help themselves to an early-morning breakfast. Carl and Brian got out the box of cereal, the bowls, the spoons, the milk. Helpfully, Carl decided to add some sugar to his little brother's cereal, so he got a jar of sugar from the cupboard, and poured the lovely red-white-and-blue sprinkles onto the cereal, then added some milk, and gave it to his brother. Little Brian ate a couple of spoonfuls, then started screaming in pain.

The "sugar" was, in fact, *Drano*™ – a highly corrosive, commonly used household cleaner. Carl's parents had to rush baby Brian to the hospital for poison treatment. The point of the story is: since the grown-up Carl intended his book to be distributed internationally, we had to forego use of the brand-name *Drano* and instead state it as "a highly corrosive, commonly used household cleaner,"

because – whereas *Drano* may be commonly known in North America – it is not commonly known in Papua New Guinea, for example. What is common in one culture may be completely unknown in another. Therefore, carefully **target your audience.**

Christianese

Related to the subject of targeting your audience is the use of "Christianese." Believers can toss around terms like "communion" or "sanctification" or "anointing" ... but do these terms make any sense to the person whose spiritual eyes are not opened?

You should no longer walk as the rest of the Gentiles walk, in the futility of their mind, having their understanding darkened, being alienated from the life of God, because of the ignorance that is in them, because of the blindness of their heart.

Ephesians 4:17-18

As Editor of that Christian magazine, initially my job was to produce a monthly magazine filled with uplifting articles, messages that ministered, testimonies that inspired. Then, as high-priced "consultants" were paid to come and re-direct the course of this thriving ministry organization, I was instructed to change the tone of the magazine to make it more of a fund-raising tool, one that specifically "influenced" readers to support this ministry with their finances. I worked with top layout artists and graphic designers, using the most popular publishing "tricks" to create a glossy,

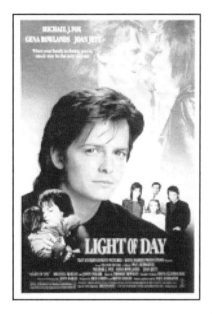

attractive magazine, with splashy headlines, lots of color photography, contemporary vocabulary. Month after month, we produced these slick magazines, and they did achieve their effect of increasing revenue for the ministry.

Then, during a vacation, I saw a secular movie, *"Light of Day,"* starring popular actor Michael J. Fox and rock-musician Joan Jett. The plot revolved around a brother and sister who grew up in a dysfunctional family, with an abusive, alcoholic father and an ultra-conservative, meek, religious mother. In one scene, the now-adult children reluctantly go home for the mandatory Sunday Family Dinner. While uncomfortably waiting for the meal to be served, the siblings sit side-by-side on a sofa in their parents' house. On the coffee table before them are artfully arranged Christian literature: books, tracts, magazines. The brother picks up one of the magazines – placed there so carefully by his mother, who desperately hopes to influence her godless children toward Christianity – and he begins leafing through it.

The camera angle was shot from just over his shoulder, so the audience could see what he is cursorily and cynically scanning ... and I was shocked to see that the magazine pages contained **exactly the same** layout, graphic and titles – the same concept of Christian literature that I was faithfully producing in the latest issue of our magazine back at my job!

I scarcely remember the remainder of the film for I sat in the theatre and numbly contemplated: *"Am I producing materials that are actually **offending** non-Christian people? Isn't what I am supposed to be doing to **reaching** those who are lost in Satan's grip, not driving them away?"* When my vacation was over, I went back to my beloved job ... and I resigned. I do not believe in wallowing in Christianese so much that I exclude the rest of the world who are hopeless without Jesus Christ in their lives in reality and power.

I am adamant about avoiding Christianese in my writing. The most comfortable Christian audience will understand what I am writing ... and so should the most remote non-Christian person who just might pick up my book and skim through it.

The Pharisees said, "Why does your Teacher eat with such scum?"

When Jesus heard this, He replied, "Healthy people don't need a doctor, sick people do. For I have come to call sinners, not those who think they are already good enough."

Matthew 9:11-13

Jesus responded, "The Son of Man has come to seek and to save those who are lost."

Luke 19:10

I believe that we are Christ's scribes, and it is better to use our talents and energy to **speak to a starving world** than to an obese Church. Remember to target your audience, and to remember **who** you are writing for ... and **why.**

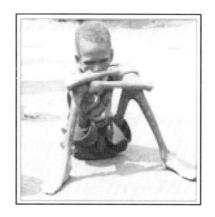

Lesson Four

(1) Think of real-life people you actually know, and put them into one of these categories:

- A high school student _____
- An elderly Christian man _____
- A young married couple, non-Christians _____
- A person not of your ethnicity and of opposite gender _____
- A teller at your bank _____
- A fellow patient waiting at the doctor's office _____

(2) Now pick **one** of these above example, and re-write the 23rd Psalm in language suitable for them:

_____

_____

_____

_____

_____

(3) What is the most significant thing you got from this chapter?

_____

_____

_____

Lettuce = leafy, green vegetable

Tomatoes = Red, round, orb of taste

Bread = loaf of fluffy goodness

Ham = the best part of a pig

Milk = the juice of a cow

Jam = garnish to peanut butter

Chapter Five: *Getting Started*

Writer's Block

Frankly, I don't believe in "Writer's Block." A writer **must** write ... something! Imagine you are on a deadline, you **have** to get this manuscript by a certain time ... and you're stuck. Don't sit there and chew your fingernails – ***write something ELSE!*** Simply writing itself can be very liberating, and can dislodge that Block.

Writers love to express themselves in a wide variety of ways. We can write out short little phrases, putting words together in a certain pattern that produces a pleasing sentence, and just scribble them in our journals for no particular reason ... and then, sometimes to our own amazement, much later we'll remember that phrase and fit it into an entirely different application than we were originally envisioning. I **never** throw away anything (call me a pack-rat) because something which is written for one purpose but not used can easily be cut-and-pasted into a different place.

"Blocked" writers should stop doing what they are "supposed" to be doing, and instead write a quick letter to a friend, or to the editor of your local newspaper, or an e-mail (my personal favorite). [Electronic mail is a great way to express something that's on your heart (as long as you aren't accused of "spamming" other people with the outpourings of your fast little fingers).] Writers can always find **something** to write about, even if it's not their intended project.

Writing something else can have positive effects (other than distracting you from that Block problem). I remember being very involved in a lengthy writing project to which I was devoting weeks and weeks of labor. It was imperative I complete this project in a timely manner with a high degree of superior workmanship. I was very focused on this project ... okay, so I am **always** focused, being the goal-oriented person I am (smile).

During this project, one Sunday morning my family and I attended church, as we always do. When the invitation to receive the gift of salvation was given, as a faithful Christian I was quietly praying fervently, interceding for all who were lost to hear the Savior's call and respond. My spirit was troubled, especially since I was aware there were several unsaved persons present ... but they simply were not responding. Specifically there was "Janet," a young woman from a very dysfunctional family, who had the reputation of being the "school slut." She **really** needed Jesus as her Savior ... but she did not respond.

The next morning, I sat down at my computer to resume the important writing project ... but I was stalled. I could not think of anything productive to write for this time-sensitive project. Instead, my attention kept being distracted by thoughts of young Janet and her Christ-less condition. Finally, I set aside the writing project, took a pad of paper and a pen, and began to write ... a poem:

Come as you are

Jesus is calling to you

Come as you are

He is reaching for you

'Though your sins are many and black

His forgiveness is just what you lack

He paid it for you

He'll make you brand new

All He asks is that you come as you are

Jesus says to come as you are.

That was it. I felt a release in my soul ... and I went back to the writing project, which then flowed smoothly. Later that day, I gave the poem to my husband – who is a marvelous musician (which I am not) – and he set the poem to music, composing a lovely plaintive melody. We produced a song intended to be sung during a salvation invitation.

The next Sunday, Kenneth (who was also a Worship Leader at our church) introduced the song to our congregation ... and to Janet (I was very glad she had returned to church!). When the salvation invitation was extended this time, Janet responded, and became a born-again Christian. Hallelujah!

I am not so foolish or prideful to think that "my song" was "the key" to Janet receiving Jesus as her Savior ... but I strongly believe it **contributed** to her life-changing decision. And I believe that the "spell of Writer's Block" was actually Holy Spirit prompting me in an entirely different direction than my intention – as in *"He who has an ear to hear what the Spirit says"* (Revelation 2:7). Eventually I successfully completed the writing project well before the deadline. Best of all, Janet remains a strong Christian woman today. And we have subsequently sung *"Come As You Are"* during other salvation invitations all over the world, with a precious harvest of souls resulting.

Writing Keys

Here are some important keys to dealing with Writer's Block and truly getting started in your writing:

(1) ***Write something every day.*** Write a letter. Write a poem. Write out your grocery shopping list using colorful expressions: instead of "lettuce," write *"leafy green vegetable filled with nutrients and beloved by rabbits"* ... or instead of "bread," make it *"today's common form of manna, that delicious Heavenly substance which sustained the*

Israelites" – and not only will you have amused yourself, but you will have expanded your writing skills. Write out your favorite Scripture in your own words. When you get into the habit of writing **something** every day, you will find your "writing muscles" strengthening. Don't make it a chore – make it a joy!

(2) These are worth repeating: ***Write about what you know*** and ***Write to a target audience.*** That

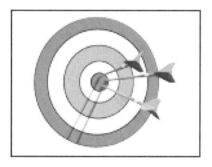

is what happened with *"Come As You Are."* As a believer, I have often extended the Savior's invitation, and I so wanted to reach Janet specifically, and it all worked together. Go through the exercise of picking a topic – if you really don't know much about it, then head to the library or the Internet, and look it up! – and then tell what you know to a specific person (or group) in language they can understand. A man can certainly write about pregnancy as well as a woman but with his own unique perspective. A woman can write knowledgeably and experientially about race cars as well as a man but with her own viewpoint represented. When you identify your name when writing an article, you are making a statement: ***"This is what I believe."***

(3) ***Become a daily journalist.*** If you don't already keep a daily journal – whether it's on your computer or in a simple handwritten diary – make the time to write out of your deepest heart. When our children were very young, my husband traveled a great deal in his business. I kept a daily journal of the activities of our weekdays so that when Kenneth return on weekends, he could spend a few minutes reviewing all the sweet little things our children had done or said while Daddy was away. Essentially, I was writing "love letters" to my husband, sharing the joy of our children with him even in his absence ... and those little books are part of my special treasures today. (Also note: I **never** use dated diaries – just lined books – because

one day's journaling may take several pages while the next day's took only half-a-page. Don't restrict yourself to someone else's predetermined limitations – the more your writing muscles strengthen, the greater your writing output.

(4) ***Make the time to write.*** If you are serious about being a good writer, you will prioritize your endeavors. There is a certain value in finding personal satisfaction in your own writing – and it can lead to a "writing addiction." The prophet Jeremiah said it this way:

If I say, "I will not mention Him or speak any more in His Name," there is in my heart as it were a burning fire shut up in my bones, and I am weary with holding it in, and I cannot.

Jeremiah 20:9

Now substitute "writing" for "speaking" and you will understand how writers become addicted to using their God-gift! It's like a coffee-lover who will not forgo his first cup of the morning – it's when writing becomes life-giving in itself. Schedule your writing!

(5) ***Always carry your writing kit with you*** – at least a pad of paper and a pen. If a "brilliant thought" hits you wherever you are, you'll be able to capture it for transfer into a different application later. **Dottie Rambo,** the wonderful and highly prolific Christian songwriter, has been known to compose some of her best songs on dinner-napkins and tablecloths. I admit that I often get great ideas in church, and the margins of my Sunday bulletins are frequently covered up and down with notes (I have my own form of "shorthand") about various writing

thoughts (but don't get the idea that I'm not paying attention to the sermon – it is "multi-tasking"). I always have a pad of those little "sticky notes" in my purse or pocket, and have jotted down excellent points that I used later in important manuscripts. Whether you use scrap paper or an iPad™, always be prepared to make the notes that will spur you to write later. Writing is never confined to "the perfect environment" of you and your computer in a quiet room. So, like the Boy Scouts' motto: **"Always be prepared."**

The "Hands" Experience

My late sister Judy Gossett and our "other sister" Reba Rambo-McGuire were the speakers at a Women's Seminar held over a three-day weekend in wintry northern Alberta; I attended it with them. Late on the Saturday afternoon, quite unexpectedly, the pastor of the host-church asked **me** to address the Adults Bible Class the next morning. That night in my hotel room, I sat on my bed with my Bible, a little electronic Concordance and a coil-bound notebook, and wrote out a couple of pages of point-form notes for a particular topic to use at the class: *"What's that you have in your hands?"* On Sunday morning, I presented the topic to the class, expanding off my notes, and the people in the class were very responsive. Nearly a year later, I took out those same notes ... and used that material to springboard an entire book on this subject!

Writing that book was a unique experiences. Kenneth and I were scheduled to celebrate our 25th wedding anniversary with a romantic trip to the beautiful island of Barbados, in the southern Caribbean. I had

intended to borrow Kenneth's laptop computer so I could use some of my "relaxation hours" to write *"What's That You Have In Your Hands?"* However, just before we departed for Barbados, Kenneth dropped his laptop while climbing a flight of stairs, and the laptop quickly went into the repair shop rather than into our luggage.

As I've previously mentioned, Kenneth loves to run for exercise and fitness, and since Barbados is a tropical island quite near the Equator, the most optimal time to run was early in the morning, before it became too hot. As unobtrusive as he tried to be in waking up and preparing to go out running, I am rather a light sleeper and was always awake before he left. In the fresh quiet of a balmy morning, I took my little notebook (the same one I had used for the Adults Bible Class on a wintry weekend in Alberta), my Bible and Concordance, and – either sitting on the balcony of our hotel room, or occasionally poolside, and once on the sugar-white sandy beach – I expanded the basic concept into a completely **hand-written** book.

Okay, it was still in a lot of point-form, with abbreviations, "shorthand" and notes to myself for other details, but I broke up the topic into chapters and sub-groups, and ended up with pages and pages of hand-writing; pages stained with mango or pineapple juice, sun-screen lotion, crisp from sea-salt and perspiration ... but I could still read them sufficiently that – when we returned from that lovely, romantic two-week vacation – I was able to transfer onto my home computer and eventually output a final copy of the manuscript. Even when the final format of the book was published professionally, I shall always treasure that little coil-bound notebook the best.

A Single Idea

Every book starts with a single idea. Once I heard a sermon series on "the sin of unforgiveness" – how it can destroy lives and even kill. Then I re-read the story of David in 1st and 2nd Samuel ... and I was riveted to the parts about Michel, the daughter of King Saul, the first wife of David. Everybody tends to look at David as the mighty warrior, the popular king, the ancestor of Jesus Christ ... yet Michel is given brief, terse, minimal treatment in the

Word:

Therefore Michel the daughter of Saul had no children to the day of her death.

2 Samuel 6:23

That cold assessment really shook me! Michel was the younger daughter of Saul. Her elder sister Merab was the one first promised in marriage to David by Saul, but the king then reneged on his promise and married off Merab to another man, Adriel. Then, to placate David, Saul gave Michel to the young warrior as his "trophy wife." Note this: *"Now Michel, Saul's daughter, loved David. And they told Saul and the thing pleased him"* (1 Samuel 18:20) ... but there is **no indication** that David ever loved Michel, other than enjoying the prestige of becoming the king's son-in-law.

Later Saul resumed persecuting David, and Michel was instrumental in helping her beloved husband escape her father's deadly wrath ... and from that moment – until it was expedient for him to consolidate his eventual kingdom – David **abandoned** Michel, and married a handful of other women. In the intervening years of his relentless persecution of David, Saul vindictively divorced Michel from David and married her off to yet another man, Paltiel – and the Bible specifically points out that Paltiel **loved** Michel, for when now-king David sent his servants to retrieve his "politically correct wife," Paltiel ran after his wife weeping (see 2 Samuel 3:16).

The more I read about Michel, the more incensed I became that she had been given a raw deal in the light of history. Yes, she was most famous for scolding David for his "inappropriate behavior" as the Ark of the Covenant was being returned to Israel (see 2 Samuel 6:16-23), but I think she had years and years of rejection, mistreatment, disappointments in her life that sparked her unhappiness and deep bitterness:

- She had been awarded as "second prize" to a man who didn't love her (and possibly resented her);
- She was forcibly divorced from the man she loved and married again against her will (but surprisingly found happiness with Paltiel);
- She was stolen back from the man who loved her and returned as a "prize of war" to the man who had once callously abandoned her.

The unforgiveness that tormented her was **not** justified, but it produced a venom that corroded her heart to the day of her death. Michel was truly an anti-heroine of the Bible, the sad definition of unforgiveness and bitterness.

I took this single idea – unforgiveness – related it to a Bible person, and wrote the novel *"Bittersweet."* It was my own interpretation of a life gone wrong ... and I offered alternatives Michel "could have" taken to prevent the destruction of her happiness and reputation. David doesn't come out as the wonderful role-model we often think of him, but he did emerge as a very human person, complete with faults ... as did poor Michel. I hope that book has served as a warning to people who struggle with unforgiveness and bitterness in their lives.

The Unique Gift of Ghost-Writing

Another aspect of getting started is that **many people never do get started** because they feel inadequate to the task. I have made a profession of being a ghost-writer for some talented people to whom God has given excellent teachings but who either feel inadequate, under-educated or

Four Generations (left to right): Jeanne (*née* Gossett) Halsey, holding newborn Alexander Halsey ... Joyce (née Shackelford) Gossett ... William Canada Shackelford, holding 2-year-old Jennifer Halsey (1978)

primarily lack the TIME to write their own books.

William Canada
Shackelford (1904-1983)

The very first book I ghost-wrote was for my maternal grandfather, **William Canada Shackelford.** *"Great Transactions of the Power of God"* told his story of an ill-educated, rough-and-tumble character who found the reality of Christ Jesus while he was a young man ... who became an itinerant evangelist and pastor in the southern United States during the early part of the Twentieth Century ... who was among the founders of the Pentecostal group that later became the Assemblies of God denomination ... who was self-taught in God's Word by memorizing huge chunks of Scripture passages, and who could preach up a storm in the pulpit.

Grandpa Shackelford told his story by speaking into a cassette-tape recorder, which a stenographer then transcribed verbatim into print. Then I took those transcriptions and put the whole story into chronological order, making it cohesive and readable.

From the first I was adamant that this book should be **by** and **about** Bill Shackelford ... so I eschewed my "education" and deliberately kept in as many of Grandpa's colorful Oklahoma idioms, grammatically incorrect as they may be. For instance, if he referred to a person as "that fella," I did not change it to "that man." Thus the book, in first person, came out sounding just like you are having a one-on-one conversation with him, with all his original flavor and zest. Even the title came directly from his speech patterns.

Feverishly, I worked on that book because Grandpa's health was failing fast. I sent the first draft to him by courier so he could have access to it as quickly as possible. Shortly after posting the manuscript, we received a phone call from the family in Oklahoma: "Grandpa is back in the hospital; come quickly." At the time, my parents Don and Joyce Gossett were overseas ministering in India ... but if Mother wanted to see her father once more before he "went Home to Glory," she needed to cut short her missionary trip and return to North America immediately. It took several days to track down Dad and Mom in India, to rearrange their flights and get them back home ... but Grandpa Shackelford hung on to life.

About a week after that emergency phone call, Dad, Mom, my then-toddler son Alexander, and I finally flew back to Oklahoma, arriving at the Miami Baptist Hospital quite late at night. When we walked into his hospital room, Grandpa was awake, but because of the debilitating stroke, he was unable to speak; he communicated with his eyes and feeble hand gestures.

I asked, "Grandpa, do you remember your great-grandson Alexander?" He looked at my little son – his firstborn great-grandson, whom he had met only once before – and indicated, "Yes." Then I asked, "Grandpa, did you read your book?" Again he nodded, his eyes twinkling. "Did you like it?" He smiled broadly, and Marmie (his wonderful wife, whom he had married after the death of my grandmother) assured me, "Oh yes, Jeanne, he really liked the book!"

"Is there anything you thing needs to be changed?" I asked. He indicated he was completely satisfied with the book. "Alright then," I was so pleased he was happy with my first ghost-writing effort, "I should take Alexander home to Sylda's, and we'll see you in the morning." I kissed him goodnight, and we retired to my aunt Sylvia's house.

Early the next morning, I heard the phone ring at Aunt Sylvia's house: Grandpa Shackelford had just died, gone to his Eternal Reward in Heaven. How glad I was that I had been able to see him one last time, and to speak with him about his book – the only one ever published for him – before he died. And I know that, when my time comes and I go to Heaven, I **will** see him "in the morning." *"Great Transactions of the Power of God"* was published posthumously, and sold very well. In 2011, I republished it.

I "Act" It Out

My "formal training" as a Theatre major is one of my "secrets" to effective ghost-writing. Just as an actor studies his role in the script to understand the personality, speech patterns and unique characteristics that bring his role to life, so it is with ghost-writing. My ultimate goal is to produce a book that does **not** sound like Jeanne nor even represents my opinions ... but truly reflects the client who commissioned the manuscript. The client is the one who has the original thoughts in on the subject – I merely help put them into a readable manuscript form. Sometimes when a chapter might seem a little short or incomplete, **with the author's permission** I will expand the material to flesh it out.

Through the gift of ghost-writing, I have been able to help others get their books finished. Taking her extensive original materials, I wrote a major best-seller for **Marilyn Hickey,** *"Break the Generation Curse,"* and I know that book ended up sounding just like her. Nearly 15 years later, I ghost-wrote two books for her daughter **Sarah Bowling,** *"Solutions"* and *"Fearless on the Edge."* It has been my privilege to help them bring their timely messages out of storage and into the lives of people around the world. I consider these books (and others) to be collaborations between what **God** wanted to say through His teamed-up servants.

Linda and Joe Knight

Procrastination is Wasteful

A very dear friend, **Linda Knight** of Monroe, Washington, wanted to tell her story of the romance with her husband **Joe** in the early years of their marriage and their life without Christ, then their truly miraculous simultaneous conversions to Christianity, and their subsequent ministry. She titled her autobiography *"My Knight in Shining Armor,"* and it was complete with Vietnam-era salty language (which she included for its authenticity), and I was honored to help her bring the excellent story into a nearly-completed manuscript.

In January 2000, who were pastoring a vibrant church, Linda and Joe took a missions team to Mexico; she assured me that she had the manuscript with her and would finalize the changes during this journey. On January 31st, flying back on *Alaska Air flight 861,* the plane began experiencing mechanical difficulties ... and subsequently crashed off the coast of California – everyone onboard was killed. Linda and Joe tragically died ... but her book still lives (although yet awaiting completion). Linda wanted her story to be made into a movie; she even chose actors to play herself and Joe.

This chapter is titled *"Getting Started."* Do not ever think you have "forever" to finally discipline yourself to start writing – as soon as you finish reading **this** chapter, **write something today.** The following Scripture is one of my favorite verses; let its truth motivate **you** today:

So teach us to number our days, that we may gain a heart of wisdom.

Psalm 90:12

Lesson Five

(1) What is the first thing you remember writing with which you felt completely satisfied?

_____

_____

_____

(2) Be honest: would you be willing to share your gift of writing with another by helping as a ghost-writer?

_____

_____

_____

(3) What is the number one thing that prevents you from "getting started"?

_____

_____

_____

(4) What are the three most important things you gleaned from this chapter?

_____

_____

_____

Chapter Six: *Make an Appointment*

Don't confuse this chapter with the previous one. Getting started is a **decision** – actually doing the writing is a **discipline.** The single most important piece of advice I can give you about this is: ***make an appointment to write.*** Just as you make an appointment to see a dentist to treat a toothache, or an accountant to work on your income taxes, or but tickets for a movie at a specific time – so you must **schedule** writing into your life.

Young Christians are encouraged to read their Bibles every day. However, very few people start out with "a complete and thorough understanding of God's Word" ... and they often fail in fervent commitment to Bible study, excusing themselves on "grounds of incomprehension." Our churches are filled with those who wear the label "Christian" but who do not strengthen their spirits on a daily basis by regular Bible study – they prefer to get a "quick fix" on Sunday at church. Most pastors can spot the members of their congregation who are daily-fed on God's Word ... and those who like to "look good" on the outside but are really anorexic spiritually.

Key-Word: Self-Discipline

The Bible is filled with verses about discipline, and the Apostle Paul wrote a great deal about it, especially **self** discipline. Why? Because most people are lazy and undisciplined! I can assure you that the diabetic who wants to stay alive will not miss his insulin medication, nor would the aspiring concert pianist miss a day away from her keyboard.

Therefore hear Me now, My children ... (Do not) say, "How I have hated discipline, and my heart despised correction! I have not obeyed the voice of my teachers, nor inclined my ear to those who instructed me!" ... He shall die for lack of discipline, and in the greatness of his folly he shall go astray.

Proverbs 5:7, 12-13, 23

Whoever loves instruction loves knowledge, but he who hates discipline is stupid.

Proverbs 12:1

Paul wrote: *"Fathers, do not provoke your children to wrath, but bring them up in the training"* – which is also translated *"discipline"* – *"and admonition of the Lord"* (Ephesians 6:4). He added: *"For God has not given us a spirit of fear, but of power and of love and of a disciplined mind"* (2 Timothy 1:7;

emphasis added). Read Hebrews chapter 12, realizing that *endurance ... chastening ... correction ... subjection ... strengthening ... training* are all related and come from the same original thought: **discipline.**

No discipline seems to be joyful for the present, but painful; nevertheless, afterward it yields the peaceable fruit of righteousness to those who have been trained by it.

Hebrews 12:11

"I have wanted to write a book for years, but I just don't seem to find the time!"

How many times have I heard that excuse? Frankly, that excuse has kept me in business as a ghost-writer! All the "helpful hints" from the previous chapter are intended to **motivate** you to start writing – but there comes the point where I can only say, *"Do what you have to do.*

Only YOU can **make** *time in your life to write.*" (But if you read through this entire book and do not start – or keep – writing, then I will have failed in my job as a writing teacher ... and shall be greatly disappointed in you. But no pressure.) (Okay, yes, lots of pressure!)

Even if you start with only one hour per day, that is a start! If you want to be a professional writer, you will need to work your way up to more than that. If you are interested in only being a casual writer, you **still** need to have self-discipline. No one becomes an Olympic-class body-builder by picking up dumb-bells just once a week or once a month. Every day, the serious athlete will take to the track, or to the gym, or to the mountain trail, or wherever, to improve his skills. Purpose in your heart not to be a "weekend warrior" but a **true writer who will not forego daily self-discipline.**

Do you not know that those who run in a race all run, but one receives the prize? Run in such a way that you may obtain it. And everyone who competes for the prize is temperate in all things. Now they do it to obtain a perishable crown, but we for an imperishable crown. Therefore I run thus: not with uncertainty. Thus I fight: not as one who beats the air. But I discipline my body and bring it into subjection, lest when I have preached to others, I myself should become disqualified.

1 Corinthians 9:24-27; emphasis added

Take notes! That is not the same as doodling idly on a piece of paper – it is training your ear to hear what others say and recording it as accurately as possible. Having a keen ear is critical if you are going to write dialogue because people may be speaking the same language, but everyone has their own unique way of communicating ... and learning to write conversation believably comes from having a keen ear and a quick hand to capture it.

Teamwork

One of my favorite things to do is to take a song learned at church and "expand" on it at home. I study the song, looking up Scriptures which relate to this subject, exploring the rhythms of the lyrics (which is not the same as a rhyme scheme), analyzing what appeals to me about that song. Whereas my husband can play the music of the song, I can always capture the lyrics quickly.

When Judy was the Worship Leader at our local church, she taught a great chorus, *"I Want to Drink From the River of Life"*:

I want to drink from the River of Life

I want to live and dwell in Your presence

I want to drink from the River of Life

Fill me with fresh oil, fill me with wine

It was a good motivating chorus, encouraging us to enjoy the presence of Holy Spirit ... but it was only a chorus (I never knew if there were verses). As I allowed that song to minister to my spirit, I found myself with a pad of paper and a pen, and the following **additional** lyrics came to me:

Yesterday's bread won't feed me today

Yesterday's prayers are not what my heart wants to say

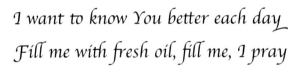

I want to know You better each day

Fill me with fresh oil, fill me, I pray

Break down my pride, my fear and my pain

In the core of my heart, revive me again

Pour out Your power, shower Your rain

Fill me with fresh oil, fill me again.

Why did I write that? Because I saw an opportunity for deeper ministry which could be explored and expanded. I was focused on a song that ministered to **me** but also had more to say for others. And – surprise! – those additional lyrics came to me on a day when I was, ahem, experiencing a teeny-tiny form of Writer's Block. Let me emphasize: as a Christian writer, **you are teaming with God's Holy Spirit** – *"He who has an hear, let him hear what the spirit is saying"* – and He **will** use you and your writing gift for His purposes and to bring Him glory.

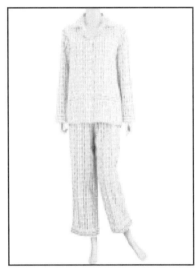

When I sit down to write, I am always conscious of **my Divine Co-Author sitting with me.** In fact, I can produce pages and pages of manuscript ... and scarcely remember their creation. That is Someone Else writing through me! (Not to be confused with hocus-pocus "spirit-writing" about which charlatans and black-magic practitioners boast – this is God speaking through me on the printed page, just as He speaks through the preacher in the pulpit.) When you are in partnership with Holy Spirit to write, making that daily appointment is a joy, not a drudgery.

My Little Secret

Here is a little secret: **I often write in my pajamas.** Sometimes I will wake up in the middle of the night with something burning within me (no, not heartburn) to write, and so I'll go out of our bedroom and fire up the good old laptop. This "bad habit" has carried over into my daytime life because I am blessed to have a job that does not require me to look presentable for the public. Therefore, with a cup of coffee (usually cold before I remember to drink it all), with my faithful dog Lucy sleeping nearby, and me in my pajamas, I often will jump into my writing day with eagerness. I actually resent needing to stop and eat breakfast or lunch – needing to halt in mid-stream the flow of creativity is difficult for me!

When you **discipline** yourself to making a writing appointment and then keeping it, you just might find yourself **addicted** to writing!

This chapter is not very long, but it contains a principle that is very powerful. Purpose in your heart **right now** to make a daily appointment to write. Soon you will find yourself being a prolific writer, and you will find yourself being one who *"strengthens the hands which hang down, and the feeble knees"* (Hebrews 12:12) for others who aspire to write.

Strengthen the weak hands and make firm the feeble knees. Say to those who are fearful-hearted, "Be strong, do not fear! Behold, your God will come with strength, with the recompense of God; He will come and save you.

Isaiah 35:3-4

Lesson Six

(1) Analyze yourself – your strengths, your weaknesses – and pinpoint those thing that previously have stood in your way of making a daily writing appointment. Address them with this attitude: *"I am going to re-prioritize my life to make room for a daily writing appointment."* Write it here:

_____

_____

_____

(2) Pray about your partnership with Holy Spirit regarding your writing. Write out a "contract" with Him wherein you agree to meet Him for a daily writing appointment. Date it and sign it:

_____

_____

_____

(3) What is the most significant thing you learned in this chapter?

_____

_____

_____

Chapter Seven: *Multiple Styles*

Several times I have mentioned alternate forms of writing – poetry, letters, songs, essays, and so forth – but here are others, for your consideration.

In addition to my colorful imagination, God has gifted me with vivid **dreams,** which I can later remember in clear detail. As children, my younger sister Marisa and I would often nearly be late for school because I took so long in telling her my dreams of the night before; now my husband Kenneth still patiently endures my early-morning commentaries.

I'm not saying I am like Joseph, with a God-given gift of dreams and their interpretations, but certainly there have been many instances when some dream has found its way into my later writings. Nor can I profess that my dreams are actually prophetic, yet I have always been one to experience a fair amount of *déja vu* (that odd sense of *"I have been here, in this situation, before"* or *"I know what is going to happen"*), so I have learned to accept the dreams God gives me, which may be given for a purpose:

Then the Lord answered me and said, "Write the vision [dream] and make it plain on tablets, that he may run who reads it. For the vision is yet for an appointed time, but at the end, it will speak and it will not lie."

Habakkuk 2:2-3; paraphrased

Mini-Script

Another favorite writing style of mine is theatrical: turning a good

story into a script. I dreamed one night about a (fictitious) man who was horribly disfigured from a wasting disease. The next day, I wrote *"The Healing of Harry,"* a dramatic radio script centered around a dying man, and the warring angels and demons fighting over his life. (*"Thanks, Frank Peretti!"*) I later turned the script into a short story.

Consider this: phone a friend and have a casual chat, but take notes of your conversation (you may want to record it, but you should get your friend's consent first). Then make a transcript of your conversation, writing it up like a script. Example:

GAYLE: Hi, Mom!

MOM: Oh, hello, dear. How are you?

GAYLE: Just fine. How's Dad?

MOM: Well, yesterday he hurt his back again, so he's trying to lay low today.

GAYLE (indignant): Was he putting up the Christmas lights without any help again? I told him I would have Jimmy come over and do that for him.

MOM (amused): You know your father! He just has to do it himself because he's the only one who can do it right!

You may surprise yourself at how quickly you learn to write a good, crisp, moving-the-story-along dialogue if you first approach it as a script.

In *"And God Created Theatre,"* I explained that while I enjoyed being an actress in college, what I **really** loved was being the director. To this day, I would much prefer directing a church Christmas play over acting in it – it's more behind-the-scenes but I have greater satisfaction (plus I have the "guilty pleasure" of getting to play **all** the parts while directing the cast).

Even more fun than directing is **writing** the script. When I wrote *"Another Chance,"* my family thought I was rather strange because I stayed locked up in my bedroom, writing furiously, and all they could hear was my muffled voice behind the door ... for as I wrote, I was acting out all the various characters, even using different voices. I **was** *Simon Peter* ... I **was** *Mary, the Mother of Jesus* ... I **was** *Joseph of Arimathea* – yet each role had unique characteristics. I learned to do that simply by writing dialogue – regular, every-day dialogue. It is good practice.

Back to School!

There are some basic rules by which all writers need to abide: those all-important rules of grammar, spelling, punctuation, vocabulary. If you feel you are not strong in these areas, don't let that stop you from being a writer – get an editor! Ask a friend to be your proof-reader (and don't get angry if they say you need to re-write). Another great way to proof-read your own work is to read it aloud. **A large portion of writing takes place all inside your mind** – getting it committed to paper (or onto your computer) for posterity, with all the correct rules and regulations followed, is part of the discipline of becoming a good writer.

I become irritated when I read something poorly spelled, grammatically incorrect or wrongly punctuated. Unfortunately, this is a common occurrence even in already-published materials, and – surprisingly – in TV commercials. Why oh why do so many people confuse adjectives and adverbs? It isn't **that** difficult ... but so many people are lazy, rather than ill-educated. My family laughs at me when they see me proof-reading and correcting the Sunday bulletin at church, but I am such a stickler for correct spelling and good grammar! Equally, I also truly appreciate an original turn of phrase!

Some years ago, the mother of friends of our passed away. They asked me to take some of her journals and glean material for her Eulogy and Obituary. I knew their mother only slightly, but I never suspected she was a great writer! The very first thing I read (from her journal) told about her last birthday, when she fell and broke her hip: *"Have you ever had a week where you wanted to flip it over and see where it was manufactured? That's what this past week has been like for me. ..."* What a privilege it was for me to write a loving Tribute to a wonderful woman like **Nancy Conklin.** You would never have known from looking at her that she was such a poet.

You can also certainly study the subject of grammar, but I find the best way to learn it is to **absorb** it through reading. Read everything you can – and pay attention to what makes sense to you immediately ... and what you have to wrestle to understand. Since writers use words as their tools, you will become more comfortable with the correct spelling of your words as you write more and more. And don't forget: there are always spell-checkers! Primarily, when you write, do your very best.

But you must continue in the things which you have learned and been

assured of, knowing from whom you have learned them, and that from childhood you have known the Holy Scriptures, which are able to make you wise for salvation through faith which is in Christ Jesus. All Scripture is given by inspiration of God, and is profitable for doctrine, for reproof, for correction, for instruction in righteousness, that the man of

God may be completely, thoroughly equipped for every good work.

2 Timothy 3:14-17

Emphasize Your Strengths

My most effective writing is applied through books, but there are other writers who have greater strengths in areas where I'm weak. There are magazine article writers ... letter writers ... script writers ... poets ... advertising writers. Be willing to explore all kinds of writing applications – **always** be willing to learn something new! – but when you discover your greatest strength, do that the most. I happen to be a very quick writer; others agonize over every single word. Whatever your writing ability, accept it as a gift from God ... and then offer it back to Him with your very best effort sustaining it.

The best thing about being a writer is that **you want to write.** Writing can easily become an addiction – but there's a Biblical precedent for that too; the previously-mentioned cry from the heart of the Prophet Jeremiah:

O Lord, You planted in me the gift of writing, and I was persuaded; You are stronger than I, and have prevailed. ... Then I said, "I will not make mention of Him, nor write anything else in His Name." But His WORD was in my heart like a burning fire, shut up in my bones; I was weary of holding it back, and I could not!
Jeremiah 20:7, 9; highly paraphrased

The Tribe of Gossett; circa 1962: Joyce ... Jeanne ... Michael ... Marisa (seated) ... Judy ... Donnie ... Don – seven reasons why Dad needed God's intervention in his life ... and why *"My Never Again List"* came about!

Give and Get Credit

When I wrote the first book with

Sarah Bowling, she initially wanted to title it *"You've Got Mail."* The overall theme was God's grace, and how He daily showers His children with it; she wanted to use a title that was a take-off of the sign-on phrase used by popular Internet provider *America On-Line* (and the title of the popular 1995 movie). I told her I thought that title was great and catchy, but it would be **very** important to acquire permissions and clearances to use the title before going to print. Subsequently, permission was not given ... and the book was re-titled *"Solutions: Grace Applications For Your Everyday Situations."* Not as catchy, but it was the right thing to do.

In 1962, my father wrote a masterful, inspirational piece, *"My Never Again List,"* and copyrighted and published it. How many times over the years – to this day! – have we seen that writing plagiarized, imitated, published without credit? It has been borrowed, quoted, re-written, copied so many times! It is wonderful God spoke through Dad to minister His truths to people all over the world ... but it would be courteous and professional if the people who "stole" it would treat him with the respect he – the original author – deserves!

Someday, somebody may think **your** writings are so wonderful, so impactful, so significant that they'll want to quote you liberally ... and you will be thankful they give you the credit for what you produced through your own hard work (and God's anointing).

Lesson Seven

(1) On a scale of 1 (worst) to 10 (best), how would you rate yourself as a writer in the following areas?

    (a)   Creativity, originality _____

    (b)   Spelling _____

    (c)   Grammar _____

    (d)   Vocabulary _____

    (e)   Speed _____

(2) What is your favorite form of writing, and why?

_____

_____

_____

(3) What did you learn from this chapter?

_____

_____

_____

Chapter Eight: *Publication* CHALLENGES

An unproven author wrote a manuscript, submitted it to a publisher; had it rejected. He submitted it to another publisher; had it rejected. He submitted the manuscript repeatedly to several publishers – at least eight times in all, I think – and everyone rejected it. Their reasons were varied, but usually something like, *"We're not publishing this kind of book at this time"* or *"Your manuscript does not fit our catalogue."*

Finally, some years after he first wrote the manuscript, he submitted it to a very small, somewhat obscure publishing house ... and they accepted it! They published the book, started with a modest advertising and distribution campaign ... **and it became a run-away international best-seller that revolutionized the industry.** That small publishing house suddenly grew large and profitable, and the author was acclaimed around the world for his originality and excellence. He has continued to write and publish many other books, and each new title is greeted with eagerness by the public.

The book? ***This Present Darkness.*** The writer? **Frank Peretti.** The original publisher? ***Crossway Books.***

I first met Frank Peretti at a Writer's Retreat in Warm Beach, Washington, in 1990. He was a witty, friendly, practical person ... and the thing he emphasized to all the writers and would-be writers at the Retreat was the **importance of *never giving up.*** He also gave us suggestions for handling rejection, which every writer must learn to master.

Particularly I remember him saying, *"Not every book you write will be a winner every time. You may begin strong at the starting-line, then lose strength as you run ... or you may be following the pack for most of the race, and suddenly burst ahead. Either*

Top: *This Present Darkness* book cover

Middle: Frank Peretti

Bottom: *Crossway Books* logo

way, you must keep trying." In later years, I met Frank again, and he remains the same humble, humorous person despite his fame and fortune.

Persistence is an extremely important trait for Christian writers to have because we don't just write for our own ego-gratification – we are using the gift God gave us, and using it for His glory. There are many encouraging Scriptures which every Christian should frequently feed into his soul when rejection and discouragement come:

Every good word in its season brings forth fruit.

Proverbs 15:23b

To everything there is a season, a time for every purpose under Heaven. ... A time to keep silence, and a time to speak.

Ecclesiastes 3:1, 8

Be ready in season and out of season.

2 Timothy 4:2b

You'll note this chapter is titled *Publication CHALLENGES* ... and I wrote "challenges" in capital letters because ***I have never had a single writing project run its full course without challenges.*** No matter how clearly the terms are spelled out in advance, there is always something that will cause snags – minor or major. Because of these ongoing challenges, I have learned never to take any of my writing projects for granted, but to expect them to be just like the "road of real life": filled with unexpected potholes and detours, and joys and satisfaction. Still, like the Apostle Paul, I *"press toward the goal for the prize of the upward call of God in Christ Jesus"* (Philippians 3:14).

The Enemy Is Watching

I undertook a complicated, major writing project with some very real, very tight deadlines. It underwent format changes, concept alterations, communications challenges, scrambling and scouring for resource materials ... and I literally worked around the clock several times to barely stay ahead of the ultimate deadline. When I submitted the final huge manuscript to the client, I attached a personal letter, which said in part:

> *As we all know, this project had been floating around your business for several years, yet no one was able to complete it ... and we know that my participation in this project has not been without a lot of bumps and thumps. So I would truly like to hear your honest evaluation, constructive criticism, and even what Holy Spirit says to you about the project now. Not all my Christian writing projects are done in an atmosphere of "celestial peace and joy" ... sometimes I am very aware that the enemy has an agenda to thwart or stop a Christ-honoring project from being completed. This was one such project –yet I am grateful for the experience.*

And that's the truth: our enemy does **not** want Christian books that will minister to and bless people around the world, to be written, published or distributed:

> *Be sober, be vigilant, because your adversary the devil walks around like a roaring lion, seeking whom he may devour. Resist him, steadfast in the faith, knowing that the same sufferings are experienced by your brotherhood in the world.*

1 Peter 5:8-9; emphasis added

This puts a new light on that Scripture, doesn't it – to realize that, as a writer, you are in the fellowship, a brotherhood of other Christian writers who have suffered setbacks and rejections, have toiled faithfully for years yet haven't seen fruit ... and to know that your writing gift is also a **ministry** which God has given you to fulfill.

Stillbirths, Miscarriages and Adoptions

I have repeatedly used the metaphor of my writing projects as birthing babies. Several of my "children" have been stillborn -- that is, they have

been diligently taken through the writing process, but for reasons known only to the clients, the resulting book was never published ... and the manuscript is still sitting silently on some dusty shelf somewhere. **Or** the client has not been honest with me, and went ahead with publication of the book without my knowledge – an "adoption."

There was the time when I accepted the project of re-writing a biography for a great missionary. The project had first been undertaken by a famous Christian writer while the man was still alive; however, it as not fully approved by him at that time, so it went onto the shelf. After this missionary's death, his family gave all the materials over to me and asked me to complete the book (now including his Home-going). It covered more than forty years of this man's life and ministry, filled with drama and the tremendous blessings of God.

The original material was excellent and easy to work with. The project took me the better part of a year – including traveling overseas for on-site interviews with the surviving family and ministry partners – but I finally presented them with a good publishable manuscript. I had utilized large portions of the original writer's manuscript – with due credit, of course – and additionally incorporated several portions of the missionary's own sermons to add color, life and authenticity to the whole story. I am confident the final product was readable and publishable.

But it was never published. That is, **to my knowledge *it was never published.*** I should add that the book was intended to be translated from English into the native language of the country where this great missionary served for so many years ... so I really do not know if the translation actually happened and the book was later published in that language. I simply do not know. No one has bothered to inform me, although I have repeatedly asked for updates.

There are two important issues relevant here: **Ethics and Legal. Ethically,** I entered into a Writer's Agreement with the family of this missionary **in good faith.** Please note that I strongly oppose Christians requiring legal intervention in their dealings, whether professional or private. If we cannot look each other in the eye and before God agree to do something – if instead we have to hide behind lawyers and their eternal paperwork and delays – then I would rather not be doing business with that person, Christian or not.

On the other hand, I have found working with fellow believers to often be the worst experience because we, as Christians, come in all flavors and degrees of integrity and commitment to basic Christian principles. In many ways, I would prefer to continue accepting non-Christian writing projects because non-Christians tend to be more business-like and more trustworthy, especially with finances. Sad, but all too true.

The other issue is **Legal.** Paul the Apostle seemed to spend a lot of his time arbitrating between Christian "siblings" about what were probably rather petty issues. Again and again he urged Christians to be fair, and righteous, and God-pleasing with each other ... but since human nature hasn't changed a drop since the beginning of Time, he knew that the only way to have lasting character improvement was through the dealing and healing of Holy Spirit.

Right up front, I submitted a basic Letter of Agreement – which is **not** a legally binding document – to the family of this missionary; both parties signed it, and we all seemed satisfied we could work together to produce a book with the intention of blessing people who read about God's exploits through the life of this man. However, when it came time for installment payments (specified in the Letter of Agreement) of the

 Writer's Fee to be paid, they dragged their feet. When the Final Manuscript was submitted, they failed to publish it within the specified time-frame (as far as I know). Eventually, I had to surrender my frustrations and disappointments to God, asking for His ability to forgive them for their negligence and untrustworthiness, and for his clarity and cleansing in my own heart if I had failed in my assignment in any way.

These "adoptions" – where a book is "stolen" from me and "raised elsewhere" – have happened to me several times ... and also to many other Christian authors, including my own father (in his early days of ministry) and my brother.

As a prisoner for the Lord, then, I urge you to live a life worthy of the calling you have received. Be completely humble and gentle; be patient, bearing with one another in love. Make every effort to keep the unity of the Spirit through the bond of peace. ... Therefore each of you must put off falsehood and speak truthfully to your neighbor, for we are all members of one body. ... Get rid of all bitterness, rage and anger, brawling and slander, along with every form of malice. Be kind and compassionate to one another, forgiving each other just as in Christ God forgave you. ... Follow God's example, therefore, as dearly loved children, and walk in the way of love, just as Christ loved us and gave Himself up for us as a fragrant offering and sacrifice to God. ... Let no one deceive you with empty words, for because of such things God's wrath comes on those who are disobedient. Therefore do not be partners with them.

Ephesians 4:1-3, 25, 32-32; 5:1-2, 6-7

A warning sign: people who don't intend to fulfill their part of the Agreement will not answer your letters nor return your telephone calls or e-mails. What should you do? Let them go. **You are only responsible for your own attitude and actions** – don't let bitterness or disappointment poison you.

For if you forgive men their trespasses, your Heavenly Father will also forgive you. But if you do not forgive men their trespasses, neither will your Father forgive your trespasses.

Matthew 6:14-15

One more example. The pastor of a large church commissioned me to write a book. When I submitted the final manuscript with the invoice for remaining fees, he never responded. I finally just let it go. A couple of years later, a friend who lived in that same city just happened to see the title of a book listed in a bookstore catalogue; she thought, "Hmm, that looks like the title of that book I remember Jeanne was writing awhile ago." My friend bought the book and sent it to me – and it **was** the very same book I had written!

This pastor had published it without letting me know ... and without fulfilling the remaining financial terms of our Agreement. How terribly sad! The book itself was not at fault – and I hope it has been an inspiration and blessing to those who have read it – but that pastor was bound to have repercussions for his un-Christlike behavior. (I later learned he had some moral failing, left the ministry for awhile, and then resumed ministering.)

My Terms and Conditions

The **hard way,** I have learned how to conduct my professional writing career. Because I believer *"a worker is worthy of his hire"* (Matthew

10:10), I do not hesitate to realistically evaluate potential projects for their monetary value in terms of my time and effort. That is, I feel completely justified in expecting a reasonable financial return for utilizing my God-given gift of writing. I have learned through trial-and-error that I should not undertake a writing project unless certain financial conditions are met in advance.

As we urge you, brethren, to recognize those who labor among you ...

and esteem them very highly in love for their work's sake.

1 Thessalonians 5:12-13

Here is an honest admission. After years of free-lancing – primarily because of the disappointments and discouragements from working with various Christians who had "cheated" me – I hung up my ghost-writer's hat. Finally, my then-pastor **Robert A. Seymour** told me quite bluntly I needed to stop feeling sorry for myself and get back to work ... **and** to be **bold** in asking for **half** of the Writer's Fee to initiate the the project, and the other half upon the timely submission of the completed manuscript. Anyone unwilling to work with me on those conditions could possible topple me back into that attitude of chronic disappointment and discouragement (and lack of trust). Pastor Bob has proven accurate, partially because he was speaking with the experience of a proven salesman (a field in which he was outstanding before entering the ministry full-time) and because he was sharing basic Bible truths. He is a very straight-shooting man!

Rev. Robert A. Seymour

(The other thing Pastor Bob did was to really motivate me to resurrect dreams. In the spring of 2000, he preached a dynamic series on the topic of reclaiming your God-given dreams; this strongly ministered to me to not let detours, discouragements and disappointments destroy dreams I've had since childhood. I always wanted to be a published writer in my own right, and to help others fulfill their gifts of writings and see their books published too. All these dreams have come to pass! So if you have an opportunity, you can thank Pastor Bob because **this** book was also created because of his encouragement and advice.)

Three Essential Areas

Back to business. The basic terms of my Letter of Agreement cover three essential areas: (1) ownership of the book; (2) the finances pertinent to the book; and (3) the publication schedule. Before I break these down, let me clarify one thing relevant particularly to ghost-writing: to avoid confusion, I use both terms of "Author" or "client" as meaning the person (or persons, or entity) who has contracted me to write a book for them -- I am the "Writer" or "Editor" but he (or she, or they) is the "Author." Understand? Good!

First, the **ownership** of the book. As a free-lance writer, I generally do not end up with any of the "rights" to the manuscript, primarily because the original content was generated by the Author (through transcripts, interviews, notes, sermon outlines, personal conversations, etc.) ... and my job is to take their original content and put it into readable form. This is generally fair ... unless I must creating an extraordinary amount of "additional original content" to flesh out a skinny book. There has never been a problem with the Author understanding and agreeing to this, especially when we have each purposed in our hearts that the chief reason we are writing this book is to make it a ministry and a blessing to others. **It is not difficult to be unselfish when we're working for the King of kings!**

Outside of "ownership," I **do** expect **acknowledgement** of my participation in the project. This can be done in a variety of ways, and what appears on the front cover may be slightly different than what appears on the copyright or information page. Examples: as a "sole author" byline (*"Name of Book"* by Tom Smith) ... as a shared byline (*"Name of Book"* by Tom Smith and Jeanne Halsey ... as an editorial credit (*"Name of Book"* by Tom Smith, edited by Jeanne Halsey) ... as a participant's acknowledgement (front cover: *"Name of Book"* by Tom Smith; copyright page: *"Name of Book"* by Tom Smith; Special Thanks to Jeanne Halsey for her participation in the creation of this book). There are several ways to do this; it is important that you are clear in the beginning about what you expect.

Next, the **financial** arrangements. I charge a Writer's Fee of a specific amount. Payment is one-half of that Fee to initiate (start) the project; payment of the second-half is due when I submit the final manuscript (completion).

There **may** be Royalty participation also. Generally, if an Author is going to self-publish, then no royalties will be paid either to the Author or to me. However, if a book is published by an entity other than the Author, then he most likely will have entered into a Royalty Agreement with the Publisher ... and I usually expect to receive a nominal percentage of **his** royalties (usually 10% of **his** royalty; that is, if he receives a 10% royalty on the retail price of the book – let's say it sells for $19.99 – then he receives $1.99 per book sold by the Publisher (most often when the Author purchases copies to sell himself, royalties are not paid on those books). However, because I receive 10% of his 10% (which equals 1% of the retail), he will be paid $1.80 per book and I will be paid $0.19 per book **from the Publisher.** (It is important this is all clearly established with the Writer, the Author and the Publisher in advance; very few Authors want to both with all that accounting and check-writing.)

I wrote a book for a client many years ago, and at the time we signed the Letter of Agreement, it was understood she was going to self-publish the book only. She did, and it became a major best-seller ... and the book was picked up by a major publisher, who slightly re-titled the book and distributed it widely. The Author then received royalties for her book which was now published by the "other" Publisher (not herself). Our Letter of Agreement disallowed my participation in Royalties because it was originally produced on the basis of self-publication. Sadly, my name was also taken off the republished book, and I have never received any part of the Royalties. Oh well ... God will balance it all out in the end. In many ways, that book became one of those "adoptions" I mentioned earlier.

Finally, the **publication schedule.** Part of the production of a manuscript which is important to the client is, *"When will it be done?"* Many of my clients are often amazed that what they had attempted to do for years and had finally given up in frustration, then I am able to produce a top-quality product in a relatively short time. For instance, I will realistically schedule a range of six to twelve weeks to write a standard-length book; however, I generally come in a week or two

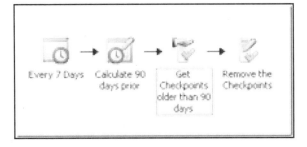

ahead of schedule – that's a win-win scenario for me and the client!

It is rare that a client truly understands schedules, especially deadlines. This is when a book project is most in jeopardy of becoming a miscarriage! *"I've changed my mind about publishing now"* is **not** an acceptable reason for failing to complete the Agreement.

One of my strongest attributes as a writer is that I am rather quick. I am absorbed in the work quite deeply and I know it is only as alive because I am making its heart beat. You could say that I instill high blood pressure to the life of the book!

As an Olympic athlete and missionary, **Eric Liddell** was quoted in the acclaimed movie *"Chariots of Fire"*: *"I know God made me fast ... and when I run, I sense His pleasure."* I feel the same way when I'm writing – especially when I'm writing quickly and the words are just pouring through me. I see words and sentences whole in my mind ... I "hear" an entire paragraph ... and I type it all at 90 to 100 words per minute, accurately. **I enjoy writing, therefore I can do it quickly – and I too can sense God's pleasure in my work!** I have worked with organizations who schedule an entire week to write a project – which I can do in a single afternoon (trust me.)

Eric Liddell (1902-1945)

Thank God for computers, for word-processing that enables us to write, cut-and-paste, retrieve, all without having to retype the whole thing over again and again. Computers and the Internet have greatly speeded up our writing processes.

When establishing a production schedule, you must factor in unknown quantities (such as an unexpected illness) so you and your client are both satisfied that the work is being performed in a professional and timely manner. As the old adage goes: *"Promise a little, deliver a lot."*

Now comes two critically important steps for successful writing. It saddens me to know too many learner-writers who have glossed over these essential rules, and later been torpedoed in their projects. Maybe this has been your own experience ...

FIRST STEP: Be certain you have ALL the resource materials BEFORE you start the project.

This primarily refers to **information-gathering;** it is possible that additional graphic materials (photographs, charts, drawings) may be generated during the manuscript production phase but those are "cosmetic" aspects and should not affect the productivity (you'll note I have used graphic support literally in this book). Again, it is the principle of having all the ingredients needed for the chocolate cake before you start the batter; the icing on the cake comes later.

SECOND STEP: Commit to a specific time-frame (deadline).

The first check-point is when you will submit the first-draft manuscript for your client to analyze (and/or approve). When I write, the first-draft manuscript is actually 95% publication-ready. The next check-point – **far too often misunderstood by the client and therefore not achieved** – is when the client has gone over the first-draft and makes whatever pertinent suggestions for changes (it never hurts to leave a little wiggle-room for the client to tinker with the manuscript). If your

client is totally dissatisfied with the product at this point – wow! You must always put your best effort into pleasing the client ... but if you have a hard-to-please client, always learn from your mistakes. In my experience, this first-draft manuscript will need a little tiny bit of tweaking to bring it into completion. So it well and do it accurately, and you will reach the last step (final draft) in no time.

There is an extremely important point that must be made: **trust between the client and the writer must be unshaken and unbroken.** When a client reads that first-draft, he may suddenly get "buyer's remorse" (meaning he begins to worry that the book is not what he wanted it to be), and then fails to return the first-draft within the deadline established. This is when most books are aborted, become

miscarriages. This single point is where Satan is most likely to insert himself into the lifeline of a book, which was birthed with the intention of being a blessing to hundreds – maybe thousands, maybe millions of lives – and so he will do everything he can to prevent that book proceeding.

It really pains me to write this because I am thinking of multiple books which I have participated in over the years and realizing how often the devil has destroyed my handiwork! Friendships with beloved persons have been crushed because that essential trust between him (the author) and me (the writer) has been lost. I am angry that the Kingdom of God has been deprived of wonderful tools – I am angry, and I'm not going to take it anymore!

An important clause in the Letter of Agreement specifically states: *"The Author agrees to* **publish the Manuscript within one year** *of the completion."* Whether the Author self-publishes or enters into a Publication contract (and negotiating with Publishers can take as long, sometimes longer, than the entire manuscript production cycle) to produce the final product, the clause has effectively eliminated (or reduced) my previous experiences of many "stillborn babies." If the Author does not genuinely and seriously agree to this stipulation at the beginning, then the negotiation is over for me – period. This may seem a little hard-nosed but it is what I require in my professional capacity as a writer.

A Handful of Suggestions

Here are a few basic suggestions about submitting your work for publication:

(1) Study the Publishers and what kind of products they make.
A Publisher who primarily issues "how-to" books won't likely be very interested in a volume of romantic poetry. A conservative denominational publisher is probably not keen on a book about your radical experiences with Holy Spirit. But do not hesitate to contact the Publisher of your own favorite books – especially if your manuscript has similarities to books written by your favorite author – because many operate on the principle of *"If it ain't broke, don't fix it"* – that is, they like to repeat successes. Publishing is first business, then ministry. This is not to discourage you from something creatively different, but it will likely save you manuscript production and postage costs if you target your Publishers according to the strongest flavor of material.

(2) Like so many areas in life, it is not always "what you know" but it is often **who you know** that will make the difference. Learn who is the current **Acquisitions Editor** at any publishing house; address your inquiries to this person, and it is less likely your manuscript will be misdirected in the mail-stream of a Publisher's busy office.

(3) Before sending an entire manuscript to any Publishers, first **send a Letter of Inquiry** (sometimes with a "sample" of your manuscript). Often the Acquisitions Editor will respond with their publication guidelines, which will enable you to determine if your manuscript meets the majority (not necessarily all) of their nuts-and-bolts. This correspondence should also produce the correct names and titles of those people who actually make the decisions about which manuscripts are accepted for publication. These are the people you want to know!

(4) Present your manuscript in the most professional way you can afford. **Bind** that book! No one wants to open a rubber band-wrapped box of loose pages, and try to keep them all in order;

invest in a 3-hold punch, use inexpensive 3-ring binders. Use **double-spacing** (although 1.5-spacing is often acceptable in longer manuscripts), with 1-inch margins (gutters) around the page. **Spell-check** everything, and make certain you have clear **pagination.** Inform your potential Publisher that you can also provide them with **digital version** (in a common software format) – they really like saving typesetting and input costs at their production level.

(5) If you receive a Letter of Rejection, write a **follow-up letter** to thank them for nevertheless giving you the courtesy of considering your manuscript ... and then ask **why** (if they have not already given you sufficiently valid reasons). Ask them if they will consider submission of future manuscripts (no one wants to take a big risk on a "one-hit wonder"), which indicates you are a serious writer with more than just one manuscript to offer. With that done, send that "rejected" manuscript off to another Publisher – remember Frank Peretti!

(6) If you don't think you can handle the negotiation phase of dealing with a Publisher, **get a literary agent** or an attorney. You are a creative writer – let someone else be the bean-counter.

Perseverance

Frankly, I have not had many happy experiences with Publishers, Christian or otherwise. Publishing is **big business** ... and I am certainly not a business-oriented person. I may not be able to tell you exactly how to overcome **all** the publication CHALLENGES you will face, other than to offer you loving encouragement, and practical support through this book.

Frank Peretti is my hero ... and so are the Prophet Isaiah and the Apostle Paul:

The Lord God has given me the tongue of the learned, that I should know how to speak a word in season to him who is weary. He awakens me morning by morning, He awakens my ear to hear as the learned. ... For the Lord God will help me. ... Let him trust in the Name of the Lord and rely upon his God.

Isaiah 50:4, 7, 10

Don't let it faze you. Stick with what you learned and believed, sure of the integrity of your leaders. ... There's nothing like the written Word of God for showing you the way ... showing us truth, exposing our rebellion, correcting our mistakes, training us to live God's way. Through the Word we are put together and shaped for the tasks God has for us.

2 Timothy 3:14-17; the Message

Getting published is a challenge. **Don't give up.**

Postscript: In the School of Creative Christian Writing, we also discuss other ways to overcome Publication Challenges.

Lesson Eight

(1) Name **three** potential Publishers. Now go to your bookshelf (or to a bookstore, or to the Internet) and get their **correct** information, including (a) Acquisitions Editor; (b) publication guidelines; and (c) contact information and/or mailing address.

_____

_____

_____

(2) Find a Bible verse that really speaks to you about your partnership with God in this gift of writing. Write it here:

_____

_____

_____

(3) What are the three most essential things you learned from this chapter?

_____

_____

_____

Chapter Nine: *Networking = Helping Others*

When I managed the monthly Christian magazine, I had on my staff several excellent graphic artists, talented photographers, sharp-witted advertising accountants, nimble-fingered typesetters, creative contributing authors, patient secretarial personnel ... and only lowly proof-reader. That proof-reader, **Judy Vanderhoof Godwin,** turned out to be my best contributing writer! Not only did she have an excellent grasp of English (spelling, grammar, syntax, vocabulary), but she could make

Judy Vanderhoof Godwin

teeny-tiny improvements to a phrase that would suddenly make the whole article pop! In her own assignments, she was interested, creative, talented – and always on time. Judy was quickly promoted to a staff writer. Judy and I have remained close friends, and she has turned her writing talents more toward television script applications. Any e-mail I receive from Judy is guaranteed to be droll and succinct.

One of the most difficult things for me to do is to give my writing to someone else to read, and then **wait** for their reaction. When I was regularly publishing *e-Jeanne* (a private-list e-mail venture that preceded blogging), getting feedback was sometimes daunting, more often humorously encouraging, but rarely outright *"Jeanne, you can write no wrong."* As much as I love my husband, rarely does Kenneth voluntarily read my work – maybe because he's learned I'll be breathing down his neck the entire time, waiting impatiently for his reaction (perhaps this conundrum is also why we have survived nearly 40 years of marriage?). As a writer, I **always** put my heart and soul into my work ... which is sometimes like walking naked in public. Even when ghost-writing – when my ultimate intent is to represent the Author's *persona* and not my own – I undertake each project with **passion.**

Three Ways to Share

The entire reason I am writing **this** book is because I enjoy helping others uncover their talents, develop them, utilize them, see them bear fruit. **Encouragement** is an important part of writing – both having people read your work and give you (hopefully, mostly) positive feedback ... and sharing encouragement free with others. A writer usually works alone – in long stretches of silence, often – and so when we come up for air, it is a good thing to share your work and to read another's writing.

There are **Proof-Readers** – who are primarily checking for spelling and grammar mistakes (which can be a very sore point with some writers) ... but also because of their own writing ability, they can offer constructive suggestions and helpful criticism. If you have earned their respect, the other writer will appreciate you extending yourself to care enough to help them make their writing better.

There are **Editors** – people whose job it is to take apart, to pare down, sometimes to rip the heart out of your writing ... and to criticize absolutely everything you've ever written! Actually, editors are **supposed** to know more than you do about what you've written ("seeing the bigger picture"), but sometimes their required changes to your work are for entirely different reasons than yours ... and often economically based. For instance, you just turned in a fantastic essay about democracy, all 1,200 power-packed words – and then your editor says, "Nice, but make it 300 words." That can be very deflating ... but often an editor has a perspective beyond yours, so you should submit gracefully.

But, as I've previously said, I **never** throw away anything ... so when you trim those 900 extra words – sighing sorrowfully for all those carefully-crafted paragraphs, sentences, phrases – do not permanently discard the original text. Save your first draft somewhere. You never know when some of that "left-over" text can be slightly modified and applied elsewhere.

Finally, there are **Fellow Writers** who are also your readers. You can share your writing before it is published with a select group of people whose opinions you respect ... but whom you know are primarily reading it just because they love to read! These people are often rather shy about offering their opinions, but when they do so with blunt honesty, it can be startling ... and productive.

This is also where you will find your most valuable **accountability** – where your writing will be critiqued (not so much for spelling, or content, or length) but more for clarity of communication. **All writers need accountability,** whether it is to keep you on deadline, to prevent you from plagiarizing, or just to let you know that someone somewhere is interested in what you write.

So let's do it – full of belief, confident that we're presentable inside and out. Let's keep a firm grip on the promises that keep us going. He always keeps His word. Let's see how inventive we can be in encouraging love and helping out ... spurring each other on.

Hebrews 10:23-25; excerpted from The Message

On-the-Job Training

As we near the end of this book, I admit I have shared some writing basics, several tried-and-true tools, some "inside" tips that might help you get started as an established writer ... but the truth is: the best kind of training for writing is **"on-the-job training."**

Just as expectant parents will read books on "how to be a good parent" or will receive advice (solicited and otherwise) of "sure-fire" methods for raising children ... they really won't know what the parenting job description is all about until they **become** parents. Becoming a

parent involves sleepless nights, learning your children's "language," making mistakes and repairing them ... and sharing that first smile with your precious child, even if it happens in the middle of the night. Writing is much the same: a learning experience, not one that can truly be taught cerebrally only. Writing must be "caught." **The best writing is what you do when you just sit down and do it.**

Put away all your excuses. Learn the basics: pick a target audience ... build an outline ... acquire your resources ... establish deadlines ... and so on – but **start to write!** If it is simply doing the classroom or homework assignments in this book, that's a start.

An expectant parent doesn't really know how he is going to react to his child until she actually holds that little one in his arms, nor does he know what kind of father he will be when that child is 10 or 20. A writer doesn't know how well his project will turn out **until he starts to write,** nor does he know what the ultimate output will be.

When our son Alex first joined *Youth With A Mission,* I did not entirely agree with their doctrine or theology, and I told him so. But as he continued to work with them and learn a great deal, I discovered they have one very important, very commendable credo in YWAM: **put what you have learned to use IMMEDIATELY.** No sooner had Alex acquired a Certificate of Completion in a course than he was turning around and sharing what he had learned with someone else somewhere else in the world. No sitting on his hard-earned knowledge, no selfishly stuffing himself with expertise ... but learning to be a "conduit of blessing" to others.

The God Gift

The more we allow God to pour into our lives – whether we're talking talents, or finances, or ministry-gifts – the more we should give **out** from those blessings. God will never let us run short or run dry. However, if we bottle it up, plugging up our "conduits of blessing" because we're worried we might be lacking, then our flow of blessing starts to stagnate and wither. This is a basic Bible principle, one which we generally apply to the way Christians handle finances, but I challenge you to read **2 Corinthians 6:10-14** all over again in the light of your writing ability:

And in this I give advice: It is to your advantage not only to be doing what you began and were desiring to do a year ago; but now you also must complete the doing of it so there may be a completion of what you have. For it there is first a willing mind, it is accepted according to what one has and not according to what he does not have. For I do not mean that others should be eased and you burdened; but by an equality, that now at this time your abundance also may supply your lack – that there may be equality.

Wow, does that speak to writers, or what? Paul went on to say:

But this I say: He who WRITES sparingly shall also reap sparingly; and he who WRITES bountifully will also reap bountifully. So let each one WRITE as he purposes in his heart, not grudgingly (fearfully, lacking self-confidence) or of necessity ("If I am a rich, famous writer, then I am successful"); for God loves a cheerful WRITER (one who ENJOYS writing). And God is able to make all grace abound toward you, that you, always having all sufficiency in all things, may have an abundance of every good work. ...

Now may He Who supplies INSPIRATION to the WRITER and SKILLS TO PERFORM THE TASK, supply and multiply the seed you have sown and increase the fruits of your righteousness, while you are enriched in everything for all liberality, which causes thanksgiving through us to God. For the administration of this service not only supplies the needs of the saints but also is abounding through many thanksgivings to God. ... Thanks be until God for His indescribable GIFT!

2 Corinthians 9:6-15; highly paraphrased and editorially emphasized

OUR TALENTS ARE THE GIFT THAT GOD GIVES US... WHAT WE MAKE OF OUR TALENTS IS OUR GIFT BACK TO GOD.
~ LEO BUSCAGLIA

That truly sums it all up. If you want to be a writer, then write. But if you want to be a **Christian author,** then surrender your writing gift to God, asking for His blessing, His overflow, for Him to be your Co-Author, and purposing in your heart to make you gift a thing which brings glory and honor to Him, bearing *"fruit that remains"* (see John 15:16).

Ask yourself **now:** ***"Who can I help? Who can help me?"*** Let your gift of writing be one you freely share with others.

Lesson Nine

(1) Summarize ALL the main points you have learned from this book thus far (no cheating!).

_____

_____

_____

_____

_____

(2) More importantly, are you using them, and how?

_____

_____

_____

(3) What is the single essential thing you learned from this chapter?

_____

_____

_____

Chapter Ten: *Being a Ghost-Writer*

After I completed the first draft of this book, the number-one critique I received was, *"But, Jeanne, you didn't tell us how YOU do that very extraordinary thing called 'ghost-writing'!"* How to answer that question ... and all the others I often hear because people are intrigued by the concept of a ghost-writer?

The best "spiritual" application I can offer is that, when ghost-writing, I endeavor to walk and walk in the "same anointing" which God has place on the client's life and ministry. The most relevant Bible parallel I can draw would be referencing Elijah and Elisha (see 2 Kings 2), when the servant of the prophet asked for that prophet's own anointing to come upon him. Although the final text of a transcribed sermon may not have all the *"Praise God!"* and *"Glory to Jesus!"* and *"Can somebody say, 'Amen'?"* phrases in it, anyone familiar with his ministry and style can almost hear those typical expressions and fillers in the distant background.

Team Work

Is it possible Paul the Apostle was describing something like ghost-writing when he penned this?

Who do you think Paul is, anyway? Or Apollos, for that matter? Servants, both us of - servants who waited on you as you gradually learned to entrust your lives to our mutual Master. We each carried out our servant assignments. I planted the seed, Apollos watered the plants, but God made you grow! It's not the one who plants or the one who waters who is at the center of this process, but God, Who makes

things grow. What makes them worth doing is the God we are serving. You happen to be God's field in which we are working.

Or, to put it another way, you are God's house. Using the gift God gave me as a good architect, I designed the blueprints; Apollos is putting up the walls. Let each carpenter who comes on the job take care to build on the foundation.

1 Corinthians 3:5-10; the Message

I don't have any exact science for it; ghost-writing is just something I have learned to do naturally, perhaps by osmosis. It is also a special gifting from God. Because I am instinctively a dramatic person – that is, from childhood I have always enjoyed playing "make believe" and acting – I bring some of these theatrical elements to ghost-writing.

In fact, I usually approach a new ghosting project the same way an actor approaches a new role: I study the person, learning (or developing) their particular speech patterns, trying to understand their thought process ... and during the actual writing phase, I am often "acting" that person. **Hearing** and **seeing** him – whether by reviewing audio or video recordings – is extremely helpful, perhaps essential, to "capturing" his personality ... and then retaining the dynamic of that personality while converting the existing material into print. I have successfully ghost-written for many people whom I have never met in person (and eventually interacting with them in the flesh is a rare but wonderful reward).

As previously mentioned, I undertook a project for the surviving family of a great man of God, a man who had died several years before. Much of the raw material they gave to me to work with was already in good literary shape, but in order for me to get into the heart of the man himself, I additionally asked for access to some of his private, personal letters, plus audios of his sermons. I spent hours just listening to him speak, sharing his heart while he was preaching. This had nothing to do with the purpose of the assignment – this was purely research to try to absorb his personality and anointing.

When I wove snippets of these teachings into the narrative of the man's life story, these were the portions that seemed to please the family the most – the parts where their father's heart was revealed. Although I never met the man, I made an effort to learn about the private person behind the public face ... and in writing his biography, I sometimes "acted" aloud portions of transcribed sermons to retain his own unique flavor in the text. It worked.

It Ain't Rocket Science

There must be other ghost-writers who have a more scientific explanation of how they do what they do ... but all I can say is, "I 'act' that person." Authenticity of personality, an effort to accurately represent the character and motives – and an occasional willingness to suspend "rules" of grammar and literary correctness, when necessary – these are the primary approaches I take to be successful as a ghost-writer. While I am well-versed in God's Word, I also strive to **not** bring my own doctrinal perspectives into ghost-writing for it is my sincere desire to represent the client, not myself, in the text. (Of course, I will not undertake any project to which I personally take great exception; that "right of refusal" is enacted before the project starts. If that should creep into the manuscript at some later stage, that would be misrepresentation of the client.)

Some people are easier to ghost-write for than others, and a choice must be made to emphasize the strength of the message rather than the animation and color (or lack thereof) of the personality). Personally, I envision the Apostle Paul probably had a brusque, perhaps even harsh personality – likely he was difficult to get along with – but he committed volumes of excellent material to paper for posterity. Conversely, I perceive Simon Peter as a very likable man, with a vigorous, jovial personality – yet his contributions to Holy Writ are minimal (but good). Each had great things to share with the Body of Christ; Paul was more accessible (and, granted, better educated) with his writings.

Of course, the underlying component of successful ghost-writing for a Christian is reliance on Holy Spirit to say what **He** wants to say. After all, both the Author and the Writer/Editor are working together with Him to  speak to God's people through writing. I once submitted a first-draft manuscript to a client, who queried a portion of the manuscript by asking, *"Where did you get that part about dying to self?"* After combing back through the raw material, I had to concede: "I think Holy Spirit wrote that part because I can't find it anywhere in the transcripts nor in our interview notes." We both could sense the Divine Author had written what neither of us could have composed ... and **that dynamic** was what made the book so effective. (Don't get carried away with that somewhat intangible "Holy Spirit factor," however, because we should always be able to substantiate what we put into print.)

Dos this answer the question? I hope so. Ghost-writing requires the writer to utilize his **ears** – to be a good listeners to the heart of the client – as well as his hands to write. Technically: I work primarily from transcripts but I usually require audio CDs from which the transcripts were derived; this way I can both hear the rhythm of the client's speech while seeing the written words on the transcript. I also augment raw materials with interviews (either in-person or by phone, or by e-mail), to ensure I am correctly absorbing the client's perspective. Absorption of personality and speech patterns ... research into the private behind the public ... the effort to remain true to the client's views ... choosing to walk in the anointing upon that person's life and ministry – these are my keys to successful ghost-writing.

Here's another interesting question I am frequently asked: *"How can you determine if a book was actually written by it's stated author?"* Check the publication page; if it says something like: *"The Best Year of*

My Life by John Smith, with Fred Jones" – this typically means John Smith (and the story of **his** life) is a very real person with a very authentic story ... but John Smith probably didn't feel qualified to write it well himself, so he asked Fred Jones to help him out (Fred being an experienced writer). In truth, I don't often ask for that kind of byline – my ego just doesn't require it.

Does It Bother Me?

Okay, I will keep answering the many questions about ghost-writing! *"Oh, you're a writer! Will I see your books in the bookstore?"*

As modestly as possible, I generally answer, *"Yes, you will see my books in the bookstore, but no, you won't see my name on them."*

This usually disappoints the person asking that question. Invariably, it is followed by: *"Does it bother you, Jeanne, that your name doesn't get on the front cover of the books you write?"*

Top: Ken Griffey, Jr.

Bottom: Alex Rodriguez

Again my answer must be, *"No, not really."* You see, the best teams in any kind of professional Sports are those known as "the whole team," not just that season's stars. For instance, here in Washington state, we have a great Baseball team called the *Seattle Mariners.* There have been many terrific players come through their ranks; in recent years, most notably **Ken Griffey, Jr.** Many years before he gained national recognition, we saw him play for the *Bellingham Bells* – one of the *Mariners'* training league or "farm" teams – and I remember hearing the men in our family (since I'm not really a Sports buff anyway – I went to the game for the family time ... and the hot dogs) saying he was a promising player. When Griffey went on to more fame, acclaim and fortune with the *Mariners,* I still thought he was just an above-average player who had good luck in the game. A few years into his contract with the *Mariners,* Griffey decided to leave for another part of the country, to be closer to his family, and so he joined a different team ... and in many ways, he began to fade out of the public eye. Still a great player, but no longer having "superstar" status.

The same thing went for **Alex Rodriguez,** a longtime *Mariners* big-shot player, who made a career-decision (for an enormous amount of money) to switch to the *Texas Rangers* Baseball team. When he left the *Mariners,* he seemed to have also left some of his best playing days behind him. (However, my husband said, "He was 25 years old at that time and his best days were ahead of him." Thus speaks a true Sports fan, so I won't contradict him.)

Top: Ichiro Suzuki

Bottom: 2012 Seattle Mariners team collector cards

At first the Seattle fans were very upset with "A-Rod" and jeered him unmercifully whenever his new team came to play against the home-town team. But then Seattle acquired a new player: **Ichiro Suzuki,** from Japan, an unassuming, quiet-spoken man who delivered terrific Baseball performances for his new team and his new fans. Hand-made signs displayed by the fans in the stands read things like: *"Our ENTIRE team are heroes."*

What is the common denominator? The **TEAM.** At best I am a mild *Seattle Mariners* fan, and I use these examples with prejudice. But they are actually the round-about answer to the original question: *"Whenever I work as a ghost-writer, I am part of a TEAM."* I have used this analogy: God is the Coach, Who trains the players and calls the plays ... the Author is the star-player, with all the moves and abilities ... and I am the water-carrier on the sidelines, who makes sure the players have all the *Gatorade* and towels they need to successfully play the game. Our game is book-writing, and our fans are the readers.

It takes team-work – people trusting each other to fulfill their individual roles so that the team wins the game (and makes the Coach proud). The best players on any team are rarely consumed by ego ... they want to be part of the entire winning experience.

The last question for this chapter was asked by a young lady; when she heard I was a ghost-writer, she looked alarmed and puzzled: *"Doesn't it bother you to be writing about spooks?"* When I explained what ghost-writing really means, she was embarrassed at her gaffe; then she asked, *"So, are you really somebody famous, and I just don't recognize you?"* I simply laughed.

As a Christian writer, learning to defer your own ego in order to bring glory to God is important. It does not bother me that you'd have to scour through the fine print to locate my name associated with many of the books I have written. ***"To God be the glory, great things HE has done!"***

Lesson Ten

(1) Identify three or four currently popular books (any genre), and notice how many will have an Author's name ... and then someone else's name in smaller print (this is common with books "written by" celebrities).

_____

_____

_____

(2) Earlier in this book was a question asking if you would be willing to work as a ghost-writer. That was a trick question ... I was seeking a **willingness** to be generous with your writing abilities and an understanding that **all** our writing is always done within the team-work of (at least) you and God. Being part of a team will make interaction with your Editor easier too. So now write your **real** answer to that question (you may be surprised that your attitude has changed!).

_____

_____

_____

Chapter Eleven: *Poetry in Motion*

You have learned about a variety of writing styles ... have read examples of my own writing experiences ... have discovered concepts of writing pitfalls and triumphs ... and have been taught some key principles about working with others to improve your own writing. Now I am going to devote an entire chapter to demonstrating just how all these elements come together.

There will be times when your writing becomes ministry **to you.**

In 2003, I began to suffer extreme facial pain from a rare (one in 20,000) disease called **Trigeminal Neuralgia,** also known as *tic douloureux.* It is also called **"the suicide disease"** and has been described as *"among the most painful conditions known to Mankind."* [The trigeminal nerve is a paired cranial nerve with three major branches, taking sensation to either side of the face in the upper (from the ear to the eye and up into the scalp), middle (across the cheek to the nose) and lower (mouth and jaw) areas.] Exactly one month after my sister Judy died, TN attacked the right side of my face without warning; it took about two months for our

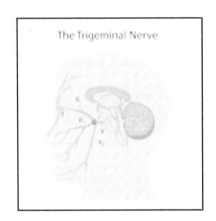

The Trigeminal Nerve

primary care physician, **Dr. James Hopper,** and a neurologist to determine the cause of the intense, relentless pain. Eventually I went on

a regimen of "Neurontin" (also known as "Gabapentin"), which is a drug given to epileptics to prevent (or control) seizures; and after trial-and-error, we found a dosage that kept the TN manageable.

Then in the summer of 2006, I woke up one day and the Neurontin no longer worked at all. Dr. Hopper dosed me with increasingly higher and stronger medications, extreme pain-killers ... but nothing was working. Unable to move my lips to speak, to eat, to swallow, I lost 20 pounds within a month. Finally I was referred (a miracle in itself; but that's a later story) to a top-rated neurological surgeon, **Dr. Kim Burchiel** (if you research TN online, you will discover that many of the "professional papers" written about this disease and its surgical repair are, in fact, composed by Dr. Burchiel). Dr. Burchiel read all the existing CT scans and MRIs, ordered a new speciality, cutting-edge, full-color, 3D MRI, and determined that he could perform brain surgery – a procedure called "vascular decompression of the trigeminal nerve" – to sever the rogue vein that was wrapped around my trigeminal nerve (I have a DVD of the entire surgery). While I was awaiting that operation, one night I got out of bed and sat at my computer to read through e-mails.

Reba Rambo-McGuire

My "other sister" Reba Rambo-McGuire had sent a message with a question about materials I was contributing to **her** Writing School, and asked for input about writing Poetry. I do not consider myself a worthy poet or much of a lyricist, but the premise of Reba's questions – about how to write to express your soul – caught my attention.

The pain from TN was so intense that it overwhelmed nearly every aspect of my life, the strongest influence on my soul had to be the 24/7 agony I was trying to endure. The bulk of my return e-mail to Reba turned into a spontaneous poem. I wrote quickly, straight from my heart, with very little subsequent revisions before I hit the "Send" button.

The point of this chapter is for you to see how a first draft morphs into a final draft, and how it often requires more than one perspective to get there.

Constructive Criticism

There are two important principles here: first is that what you write out the first time is most likely going to be at least 95% of what you will end up with. In other words, the more confident you become as a writer, the more likely your first effort will be truest. The second principle is that once you have become accustomed to writing and feeling comfortable with your abilities, then you can indulge in that **other** habit which most writers have: **incessant tweaking** or fine-tuning. Very rarely are even the most experienced writers ever truly satisfied with their work. Every writer I know can always find

something they wish they had changed before it went to print. This isn't vanity or even perfectionism – it is just knowing that what you are crafting is worthy of improvement.

Working with other writers is one of the best ways to improve your own skills. "Constructive criticism" is the key-phrase, and requires large doses of **respect** and **trust** from both parties. It starts by meeting on level ground, writer to writer; it can proceed to a different shape – such as writer to editor – but you'll find that the best input you will receive – **and** be willing to implement – comes from your peers.

Background

I have known Reba Rambo-McGuire since we were teenagers; we have a lot of history together. Reba is the only child of the late Gospel Music legend Dottie Rambo and the estimable Buck Rambo. Dottie has penned some of the greatest songs of the last 50 years and more: *He Looked Beyond My Fault and Saw My Need ... I Go to the Rock ... Sheltered In the Arms of God* – songs which have been recorded by everyone from Elvis Presley to Dolly Parton to Whitney Houston. It could have been daunting for Reba to attempt to write her own songs in the shadow of her famous and well-respected mother, but not so! Reba is a very talented songwriter, and has penned a number of well-known, award-winning Contemporary Christian songs (both as a solo writer, and with her husband Dony McGuire): *Lift Him Up ... A Perfect Heart ... The Land of Oohs*

Reba with her parents Dottie and Buck Rambo (about 1970)

Dony McGuire and Reba Rambo McGuire

and Aahs ... Because of Whose I Am. (Reba has promised to sing at my memorial service if she can remember all the lyrics to *Sparkling Gold.*)

It could have also been daunting to me to share my writing with Reba, but we genuinely consider each other "fair game" as sisters; as a teenager, Reba was glad to be "adopted" into the big and boisterous Gossett Family, and short of some sort of formal adoption process, we couldn't be closer. Yes, we've had our ups and our downs, our ins and our outs – just like any "blood" relative does – but there is nothing that will separate us this side of Heaven. Sister to sister – perhaps even more importantly since Judy's death – and writer to writer, we are loving, trusting and respecting peers.

Work In Progress

Now watch the writing process being honed as we worked together. This e-mail exchange took place in the summer of 2006; be aware that Reba lives in Nashville, Tennessee, and I live in Blaine, Washington – we are three time zones apart (she is ahead of me by three hours). Reba is more of a night-owl, but I was struggling with pain around midnight ... and she was still wide awake on her side of the continent. (Many writers are most effective at irregular hours.)

REBA: I'm getting ready to teach my Writing Class again. Do you have any favorite poems?

JEANNE: The thing about Poetry and me is that I don't think I'm a very good poet, or possibly I didn't have Poetry presented as my favorite style of writing. I like to see action, a story being told, activity, progression ... whereas I tend to see Poetry as being a lengthy discussion of the color of a leaf lying on a bench in the park in the sun. Not doing anything, just lying there. Pretty. Just lying there. I know that's not really true, because I want to know where the leaf was before it got to the bench. How many times it almost didn't make it to the bench. What little kid chased it as it swirled through the air. And then what happened when it blew off the bench. And how it got stuck on the leg of a deer, and was carried out of the park into the woods that night. And then what happened next? To me, **that** would make an epic Poem!

A true poet would enjoy describing the veins on the leaf, the varying colors of the leaf, how the shades on the upper right side are slightly different than the shades nearer the lower left side of the leaf. How the shadow on the back of the bench was imprinting the overlay of technology onto the purity of nature. She would write about the glory of the life of the leaf, yet the juxtaposition of the life of the leaf was over since it had already detached itself from the tree. How the leaf would soon wither and become a crumpled piece of dust. Sigh. All in perfect rhyme and meter.

The only reason I am moved to think of Poetry at all is because I saw something on Dr. Kim Burchiel's website [the neurosurgeon who would perform the Trigeminal Neuralgia procedure] that showed him performing the surgery on another patient. I saw him lifting the trigeminal nerve away from an offending vein which had crossed over it, and he inserted (for lack of a better explanation) a "brake pad" (usually something silicone) to relief the pain. When I saw that, I said in my heart: *"Give me, oh, give me / Tell me not of fear!"* – a quotation I'm pretty sure Judy Anne would have instantly recognized as Juliet's declaration in *Romeo and Juliet* Act IV, Scene 1 (where Juliet tells Friar Lawrence she is not afraid to try anything, even to take a "temporary poison" if it would help her escape an unwanted marriage and restore her to her true husband, Romeo.) That is the only single line of Poetry I could quote, could paint a single frame upon; otherwise it's the entire story that I thrive on. I am quite familiar with *Romeo and Juliet,* for what good is Shakespeare unless you know the

Olivia Hussey as "Juliet" in Franco Zeffirelli's *"Romeo and Juliet"* (1967)

whole Play? Couldn't you imagine a Eugene Peterson version of *The Merchant of Venice?* Staggering!

Sadly, there just aren't enough people around to share my appreciation for applying artistic or literary references to every-day life. Case in point: last night I sneezed, but the agony of a simple sneeze played havoc on the right side of my place. I toughed it out, as I must do. In the aftermath, when the pain finally subsided, I muttered to Kenneth, *"Crouching Tiger, Hidden Dragon."* He wasn't understanding until I explained, "My face, Kenneth. My face has a crouching tiger in it, a beast who likes to flex its claws. It has a hidden dragon who likes to sear with fire. From the outside world, you can't see its handiwork."

His response? "Sometimes you scare me!" If I don't laugh at myself, if I can't show that I am bigger than the problem – but if I don't have anyone to laugh with me, well, goodness! I may as well try to write a poem about it.

First Draft

There is a dragon that thinks it can live on one side of my face
Can burn and slash and break
Tracing along the lines of the nerves whenever it chooses
Just because it can, whenever it wants to do it
On a whim
Without warning

It uses the hilt of his fiery sword to crash down on the base of my nose
And then marches all the way up into my eyes
Tracing a streak with the tip of the sword
A pattern of slashes that spread out into the cheek

It always amazes me that there is absolutely no outward evidence of this gruesome parade
No dripping blood, no shards of skin hanging, no trembling tissue
Nothing to show for this dance

Sometimes this dragon uses its sword like a thousand little toothpicks
Tingling hot fires along the base of my eye, out toward my ear
Slowly, slowly drawing the shape of my face
A map that would please a biology student
The dragon in my face

There are days and days when I cannot brush my teeth
And then when I can, it is like an enormous triumph
There are days when the most gentle washing of my hair can make my whole face burn
And I just stand in the shower and weep
There are days when swallowing the pills they call pain-killers (and I call poison)
Are nearly impossible because swallowing them with the merest sip of water
Is the biggest challenge of all
Trying to coordinate the movement of water past the pain of the lip and the muscles or the mouth and throat

The dragon in my face has interfered with my life so much
And has stolen so much from me
And I am very, very angry with it
My beautiful little granddaughter does not know yet that the dragon has stolen kisses from her
She doesn't realize that Grammy has not been able to even smile at her as readily as I want
Or that she has bumped her little face into mine by mistake a few times that has really caused agony

But I am determined she will never have to understand what has been

my problem
I am going to get my life back!
And this dragon is going to be uprooted from my life for good
Because I have a Healer coming to my rescue
I have friends – just like in Mark chapter two
Friends who took their friend to see Jesus the Healer
So I too have friends who are taking me to see
A healer who is expert in his field
And I believe that even as the surgeon lifts his hands to perform
his skills
So will the Master Surgeon superimpose His hands over the natural surgeon's hands
And my healing will be completed
And the dragon in my face will be vanquished
Poof!

The End

Feedback

REBA: Okay, I'm an official mess! Your transparency and vulnerability cut to the heart. I have a favor to ask: I want to talk about "Poetry as Healing and Venting" in one of my Writing Classes? May I use your letter (at least, most of it) and your poem as an example for their notebooks? It is so raw and real ... maybe you should consider adding a Poetry Hat to your growing collection.

I think your simple poem is a great idea, a wonderful example of venting and healing through Poetry. And I'm praying harder and with much more knowledge of your pain now.

You have a natural propensity to use soft rhyme, which is fine ... except, as a songwriter, I'm a stickler for pattern. I like matching, or close to matching, the syllables in the verse. So let's say the first stanza ends with: *"A map that would please a biology student / The dragon in my face."* I would try to somewhat match the next stanza to that existing pattern. I would at least try to be as close to the same rhythm and tempo. Most poems have a natural beat. Of course, this could certainly be Prose, which can be so many things.

The re-write is so much better, except I'm not buying the last stanza – it's too neat. I understand the "snake biting the tail" principle, but it doesn't work for me here. I like *"Dragon Slayer,"* but I would perhaps use it earlier, possibly instead of *"Master Healer."* I love ending with *"Poof!"* But *"The dragon in my face would be removed"* – I think *"removed"* is way too nice a word for such an intense enemy.

Okay, I messed with this:

> *When I defy it and try to eat more than a sip of soft soup*
> *It roars with anger-swoops*
> *And belches fire consuming flesh from mouth to nose to forehead*
> *Just because it can, whenever it's evil wings spread*
> *Acid pain*
> *Purgatory.*

Of course, all this from a girl who can't spell or type. Do you hate it?

Final Draft

Reba and I continued to dialogue with this concept, and it remained a poem (not a song) ... and became the inspiration for the book I wrote about the whole experience of battling – and eventually conquering! – Trigeminal Neuralgia that summer: *"Exit the Dragon: Modern Medicine Meets Fierce Faith."* Here is the final product:

There is a dragon that thinks it can live
On this one side of my face
Can burn and slash and break
Tracing along the lines of my nerves whenever it chooses
Just because it can, whenever it wants to do it
On a whim, without warning

It parks its jagged haunches on the
base of my nose
Curls its long treacherous trail
around my lips
And then stretches its scaly body all
the way up into my eyes
Parking its cruel snout above my
forehead
Slapping its stinging tongue up into
my hairline with a hiss
Digging a chasm with its claws
An irregular pattern of slashes that
spread out into my cheek

It always amazes me there is absolutely no
Outward evidence of this gruesome gouged-out ditch in my face
No gushes of blood, no shards of skin, no trembling tissue
Nothing to show for this cruel dance

Sometimes this dragon uses its claws
Like a thousand little toothpicks
Tingling hot fires along the base of my eye, out toward my ear
Slowly, relentlesssly, drawing the shape of my face
A molten map that would please an anatomy
student

When I defy it and try to eat
More than a sip of soft soup
It roars with anger
And belches fire that consumes all flesh from
mouth to forehead

From nose to ear
And the throbbing living flesh that is my face
Is certain to suffer for hours and hours
Except there is still no external evidence
No flushing, no redness, no scarring
Nothing to indicate the internal agony
Nothing but the absolute stillness with which I hold myself
To wait it out
Wait, wait, wait for the pain to subside
Until I am so tired that I simply go to bed
And try to sleep, no need to eat, just sleep
Away from the dragon in my face

There are days when I cannot brush my teeth
Then when I am able, it seems like an enormous triumph
There are days when the most gentle washing of my hair
Can make my whole face burn
And I just stand in the shower and weep
There are days when swallowing the pills they call
Pain-killers (and I can poison)
Are nearly impossible because swallowing the merest sip of water
Is the biggest challenge of all
Trying to coordinate the movement of water past the pain
In the lip and in the muscles of the mouth and
throat

The dragon in my face has interfered with my life
so much
And has stolen so much from me
And I am very, very angry with it
My beautiful little baby granddaughter
Does not know yet that the dragon has stolen
kisses from her
She doesn't realize her Grammy has not been
able
To even smile at her as readily as I want
Or that she has bumped her little face into mine

Jeanne's granddaughter Ava
Freeman, born 2006

By mistake, which has caused agony
But I am determined she will never need to understand
That her soft little hands on my cheek have been a problem

I am going to get back my life!
And this dragon is going to be uprooted from my life
For good
Because I have a Healer coming to my rescue!
I have friends -- just like those in Mark chapter
two
When friends took their loved one to see Jesus
the Healer
So I too have friends who are taking me
To see a healer who is an expert in his field
And I believe that even as the surgeon lifts his
hands
To perform his skills
So the Master Surgeon – the Dragon-Slayer – will
Superimpose His hands over the natural
surgeon's hands
And my healing will be completed

And the dragon in my face will be removed
Poof!

Yes, I realize that once the dragon is gone
It will take time for the actual scars beneath the visage to heal
There will be days or weeks or months before
The dragon's damage of my nerves will be restored
If they ever can be
But I will laugh because
The dragon will be slain
Heh
I will always remember the dragon
And so will I thank the Dragon-Slayer.

My poem was written because I never want to forget that summer of pain, nor Who walked through the Valley of the Shadow of Death with me throughout those days. I will always remember the family, friends and loved ones He brought alongside me on this journey, who encouraged and prayed with me, and even wept with me.

The purpose of repeating this poem in this book is to illustrate the principle of revealing my poem-in-progress to a writer whom I esteem, and to show how together we improved the first draft into an excellent final product. Do you see the team-work?

Lesson Eleven

(1) Do you ever feel intimidated by someone else's writing? Have you ever worked up courage to approach him or her, and – beyond getting an autograph or behaving like a groupie – ask for constructive criticism of your work? If given an unlimited opportunity to do so, who would that writer be, and why? Write out your heart's desire:

_____

_____

_____

(2) (This might be a tough one.) Imagine someone you know and love, who has died unexpectedly. Write what you wish you had said to him or her, perhaps what you would have written in a greeting card. Don't make it lengthy.

_____

_____

_____

(3) What have you learned in this chapter?

_____

_____

_____

Chapter Twelve: *God Versus Ego*

You thought we are finished? Almost! This last topic is the heart of writing for me: **I write for the Audience of One.**

That, as it is written: *"He who glories, let him glory in the Lord."*
1 Corinthians 1:31

Thus says the Lord: *"Let not the wise man glory in his wisdom; let not the mighty man glory in his might; nor let the rich man glory in his riches. But let him who glories, glory in this – that he understands and knows Me. That I am the Lord, exercising loving kindness, judgment and righteousness in the Earth. For in this I delight,"* *says the Lord.*
Jeremiah 9:23-24

"You are worthy, O Lord, to receive glory and honor and power; for You created all things, and by Your will they exist and were created."
Revelation 4:11

I never know precisely where the words I write will go, into what hands my books will be placed, what person is going to read my magazine article or blog. I am a Christian writer in a secular world, and I have an obligation to be the best at my craft that I can be, and especially to use my talent to point people to Jesus Christ. I do not write for my own ego-gratification – I write to please my King.

And moreover, because the Writer was wise, he still taught the people knowledge; yes, he pondered and sought out and set in order many proverbs. The Writer sought to find acceptable words; and what was written was upright - words of truth. The words of the wise are like goads, and the words of scholars are like well-driven nails, given by one Shepherd. And further, my son, be admonished by these. Of the making of many books there is no end.

Ecclesiastes 12:9-12a; paraphrased

And there are also many other things that Jesus did, which if they were written one by one, I suppose that even the world itself could not contain the books that would be written.

John 21:25

Hot Hands

In *"What's That You Have In Your Hands?"* I shared this true story:

In 1987, at Wally and Marilyn Hickey's "Happy Church" in Denver, Colorado, I was asked by Evangelist Benny Hinn – a long-time Gossett family friend, who was guest-ministering at Happy Church – to assist him in the Prayer Line. Suddenly, at one point during the healing ministry, Benny whirled around and grabbed both of my hands in his and began to pray over them. Immediately my hands felt red-hot as Benny prophesied, "These hands shall write books that will touch the lives of millions of people around the world, pointing them to Jesus Christ!" My hands were made for the service of God ... and, as a writer, I have written many books.

When I first taught the Writing course at Nairobi Pentecostal Church (South) in 2000 – where, by the way, they gave me the honorary KeSwahili name of *"Mwana Hadithi,"* which means "honored story-teller"

– I was privileged to conclude the class by personally laying my hands upon the hands of every student there, praying for them, sharing what words God spoke into my "ear." During the class, I had "empowered" them by sharing the knowledge and benefit of my experience ... now I "ministered" to them through prayer and the leading of Holy Spirit. If God should create

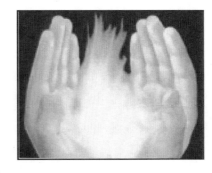

an opportunity whereby you, dear Reader, and I are in the same place at the same time, then it would be my honor to pray for you too.

Therefore I remind you to stir up the gift of God which is in you through the laying on of my hands.

2 Timothy 1:6

If, through this book, your "pilot-light" has been ignited, and soon your writing talent will burst into full flame, then I have accomplished what I set out to do. Praise the Lord!

Let me leave you with this poignant thought:

I cannot wrote a book commensurate with Shakespeare, but I can write a book by me.
– Sir Walter Raleigh

Sir Walter Raleigh (1554-1618)

Supplemental

Classroom Assignment

Paraphrase a brief passage of Scripture – such as Psalm 1:1-6 or John 1:1-5 – **but first** choose an audience of (a) children ages 6 through 12; (b) parent to child; or (c) secular application (think "Bill Gates" or "a movie star"):

_____

_____

_____

Homework Assignment

(1) Write an Essay (1,000 to 2,500 words) on: (a) *Why I Want to Write;* (b) *A Bible Story;* or (c) *My Favorite Person.*

(2) Pick an accountability partner – someone with whom you will share the formative stages of this project, who will help you establish realistic goals, and who will critique your finished work.

(3) Also send your completed Essay to me (via e-mail – halseywrite@comcast.net – or post – 4424 Castlerock Drive, Blaine, Washington, 98230, U.S.A.) because I would love to read your work (and to know how this book has equipped you).

   God bless you!

The End

Open House

Do you remember in school when, usually part-way through the first semester, there would be an "Open House"? The teacher would have the "best" of all her students' output – artwork, essays, science project, or another example of exceptional class-work – all displayed for proud parents and guests to wander among and enjoy. Admittedly I am a proud teacher of outstanding students – many who have continued on as professional writers – so I am sharing a mere handful of their class-work relevant to this book. Everyone got an "A" for excellent and effort! (Okay, so I don't grade on a curve :)

From Lesson 4: The Paraphrase of Psalm 23

For Carol, a teller at my bank:

The Lord is my Protector, my needs will be met.
He gives me a break from my labor.
He gives me peaceful sleep and He assures me of my emotional well-being.
He guides me in the right direction so I can see that I can trust Him.
Even in my fears and doubts about the future,
You will reassure me You are always by my side.
Your arm is around me continually,
And Your hands caress my face.
You make a romantic dinner for me without worrying about the cost.
You treat me like royalty,
And I will always be provided for above what I could need.
I can trust You to be good and kind to me, even when I am an old woman,
And our marriage will never die.

[Wow, this is a cathartic exercise! I teared up at *"Your arm is around me continually."* Let's do another one, with someone opposite!]

For Eric, a High School boy:

The Lord is my personal Coach.
I won't be unprepared.
He gives me the perfect playing field,
And makes sure there's plenty of water to drink.
He heals my injuries, and looks out for my best interest for my future career.
Even if I lose a few games, I can still make the playoffs;
No opponent is that scary 'cause You've given me the secrets on how to beat them.
You throw me a party after the victory, while the other teams watch.
You present me with the MVP trophy; I have more than enough options.
I'm sure my friends will be impressed.
And I won't get kicked out of school for the stupid stuff I do sometimes.
I will graduate with honors, and be successful with Your help.

[This is **fun,** Mrs. Halsey!]

– Bryan D.

To the High School Senior:

The Athletic Director is my Coach. He makes sure I know the game plan and am fully prepared. He makes sure I have all the right equipment and that it fits well. There will be no lack in my training, and I know my place in the lineup. He keeps me on the field doing drills until I know how to play my position. When I get called into the game, my team-mates are a force around me, and protect me. When the other team beats us, my Coach is in the locker room, encouraging us, and reviews the game plan with us.

He even supervises my nutrition to keep me healthy and full of energy for both the practices and the games. He sets my course so I can do well and move on into the next phase of my life. My Coach keeps working with us to bring us to a winning season. Then we can go on to win the area championship with a record that will be unbeaten.

– Darda B.

To my non-Christian siblings who are hurting:

The Lord, the One Who created you, is your Shepherd, for you are His sheep. You should not want anything that does not glorify your Lord. Your needs will get met, and that should be satisfying enough to still call Him Almighty and a perfect, loving God.

He will bring peace into your lives, and guide you into doing what's right for the sake of His Name, so your motives will stay pure. He will breathe into your soul peace and fulfilling happiness that cannot be experienced anywhere else, in any other way.

Even though life will still have difficult moments and very hard times that seem endless and pointless, don't worry because God promises to be your Advocate through all matters, great to smallest of problems. What He provides will be enough for you to deal with it, whatever it may be. Physically, financially or emotionally.

Surely goodness and love – perfect, untainted, non-biased love – will follow you all the days of your life. Those who endure to the end in the truth will go to Eternal Peace forever.

– Dori G.

The Lord is my Guide and I need not worry. He calms my soul and gives me peace when I am restless. He knows what is best for me and guides my paths to be more pleasing to Him.

I will face many challenges and many dark times. I need not fear because I will be comforted in Your arms. I will be victorious over my enemies. You will bless me with an abundant life.

– Joy R.

For the Dancer:

My Dance Teacher helps me a lot. She knows every move that I need to learn. She gives me graceful dances and fun music to move to. Between relaxing stretches to renew my muscles and showing me new tips, I can tell she cares.

*I show her my appreciation by learning all her instructions with enthusiasm and laughter. Sometimes I will stumble at a recital, but I won't let myself get **too** embarrassed because I can always see her perched in that front row seat, with a glowing smile and understanding nod to encourage and comfort me.*

*She helps me improve with hordes of good advice. Her compassionate nods chase away any hurt or shame. She knows me with harder songs, trusting in my abilities. I'm **so lucky** to have a good teacher like her! I bet her guidance and never-ending support will always be there to help me out when I need it. Every recital or practice, I will always have her there, as long as I dance.*

– Courtenay S.

For an Elderly Man:

Your LORD is your Primary Caretaker. You will have all you need. He will give you rest for your body. He will walk beside you and quiet your anxieties. He will make your soul rejoice. He will show you right way to live, and it will please Him.

When days of grief come into your life, He will never leave you or forsake you. He will protect, guide and comfort you. He will put good things before you as unbelievers look on. He will protect your mind with His Holy Spirit. Your inner joy will be endless.

His kindness and forgiveness are there for you, all the days of your life. Then your Lord will take you home to Heaven; and you will be there with Him forever and ever.

– Joan V.

Resources

Jeanne's Letter of Agreement

Over the years, I have tweaked a very workable "Letter of Agreement" that enables me to be an effective ghost-writer, giving assurances to my client that I'm going to do the work professionally and excellently, while also detailing a timetable of production. This one works for me; you are welcome to adapt it for your own use.

Letter of Agreement

This is an Agreement between NAME (hereinafter "Author") (and such agents or representatives designated by the Author) and Jeanne Halsey (hereinafter "Writer") for the Book Project tentatively known as "TITLE."

I.   Manuscript Fee

A Manuscript Fee of $AMOUNT shall be paid to the Writer, as follows:

  (a)   Initiation: A non-refundable deposit of $HALF to initiate the Project; and
  (b)   Completion: The balance of $HALF at the submission of the Completed Manuscript.
  (c)   All funds are to be paid in American currency; payable to: MAILING ADDRESS.

II.   Ownership

  (a)   The Completed Manuscript shall be owned entirely by NAME (Author).
  (b)   The By-line on the front cover of the book shall read: "By NAME"; and on the title page it shall read: "By NAME, with Jeanne Halsey."
  (c)   It is the Author's responsibility to have the book published, advertised and distributed within one year of the acceptance of

the Completed Manuscript; and there shall be an annual reporting to the Writer of the sales progress of the book.

III.   Royalties

(a)   If the book is self-published (that is, by the Author or his representative, not with a professional publishing house), there shall be no royalties paid to the Writer; or

(b)   If the book is immediately or within 5 years published by a Publisher or agency other than the Author (or his representative), then a Royalty of 10% of the Author's Royalty shall be paid to the Writer; such Royalty payment and sales accounting is the responsibility of the Publisher (not the Author).

IV.   Timetable

Upon receipt of the raw materials [existing manuscripts (such as books, magazines, newsletters), transcripts, CD-ROM disks, additional audio and/or video materials, available upon request], the Writer will utilize these raw materials to glean topical textual data for incorporation into the book.

(a)   The Writer will produce the First Draft Manuscript within 90 days of the initiation of the Project.

(b)   The Author will have 15 days to review the First Draft Manuscript, then return it to the Writer for completion; such completion will generally require 15 to 30 days, resulting in the Completed Manuscript (ready for publication).

(c)   The Writer shall be available to consult with the Author's publishing staff, with suggestions for style and presentation of the finished book.

(d)   The Completed Manuscript will be delivered to the Author as two bound print-outs and a CD-ROM.

V.   Expenses

All reasonable incidental expenses (travel, accommodations, resources, courier services, etc.) are the responsibility of the Author.

(a)   Should it be necessary for the Writer to travel outside her normal office in the course of the preparation of the book or to perform additional tasks at the request of the Author which are directly related to the preparation or completion of this book, and such activities would constitute "extra" time and expenses by the Writer (example: to interview the Author, and/or any persons suggested by him), all extra costs, charges and fees to fulfill those additional activities would be mutually discussed and agreed upon in advance of their performance, and are the responsibility of the Author; and a *per diem* rate of $PERDIEM shall be paid to the Writer, when applicable.

(b)   A full accounting (with receipts) for all manuscript preparation expenditures will be given by the writer to the Author upon request.

VI.   Complimentary

10 complimentary copies of the published book shall be given to the Writer.

Dated, signed, witnessed, and blessed!

About the Author

Jeanne Halsey is a daughter, sister, wife, mother, grandmother ... and a writer. Third of five children born to international missionary-evangelist **Dr. Don E. Gossett** and his late wife **Joyce Shackelford Gossett,** Jeanne naturally inherited her father's gift of writing (he has published over 120 books, including the best-selling *"What You Say Is What You Get"* and the ever-popular *"My Never Again List"*). Jeanne was born in Oklahoma ... immigrated to Canada at age 7 ... was educated in British Columbia (*Douglas Junior College, University of British Columbia*) ... and has resided in Oklahoma, Oregon, British Columbia, Washington state, Texas, and Colorado. She has traveled internationally extensively.

Formerly Managing Editor of two internationally-distributed monthly Christian magazines, Jeanne is now a freelance writer. She has ghosted and published books for several renowned Christian ministries and contemporary personalities: for her father ... **Reinhard Bonnke** ... **Sarah Bowling** ... **U. Gary Charlwood** ... **Frank Colacurcio** ... **Marilyn Hickey** ... **Danny Ost** ... **Paul Overstreet** ... **Cliff Self** ... **Robert Tilton** ... and **many others.** She has written for Christian and secular trade magazines, and has published several Sports articles about National Basketball Association superstar **Luke Ridnour** for *Sports Spectrum* Magazine (a division of *Christianity Today*). She also publishes an Internet newsletter *"e-Jeanne,"* and frequently teaches the *School of Creative Christian Writing,* using her book *"The Legacy of Writing"* as the curriculum.

Jeanne lives in Birch Bay, Washington, with her husband (since 1974) **Kenneth Halsey,** Vice President of Franchise Sales, Western Region, for the *Realogy Corporation;* and their empty-nest home includes two Chihuahuas, **Lucia Gracias Royale** and **Juliet Diva Royale,** mother and daughter. Their beautiful daughter **Jennifer** is married to **Patrick**

Freeman; they have two children, **Kristian** and **Ava;** and thankfully the Freemans live very nearby, in Blaine. Their talented son **Alexander** is married to **Cherry Ruth;** they have three children, **Jude, Aja** and **Hayley;** but the younger Halseys live halfway around the world, stationed in India as missionaries with the *Life-Giving Network,* an outreach ministry of *North County Christ the King Church.*

An outspoken activist for Christian causes, Jeanne has stood for public office (she lost); she is past-Chair of the Board of Directors of the *Whatcom County Pregnancy Clinic,* and past-Secretary of the Board of Directors of the *Greens at Loomis Trail Homeowners Association.* Jeanne and Kenneth are active members of *North County Christ the King Community Church* in Lynden, Washington.

"I have no idea what I said that was so funny!" Jeanne at home early one morning, with four of her five grandchildren (left to right): Aja Halsey ... Hayley Halsey ... Ava Freeman ... Jeanne ... Jude Halsey. (Summer 2011)

Other Titles by Jeanne Halsey

✳= available through www.lulu.com, www.amazon.com or www.halseywrite.com

Non-Fiction
for other Authors

- *Break the Generation Curse* for Marilyn Hickey
- *The Church Alive in Shanghai* for Paul Crawford and Bishop Aloysius Lu-xian
- *Courage: How to Make Things Happen* for Cliff Self
- *Fearless On the Edge* for Sarah Bowling
- *Follow the Yellow Brick Road Workbook* with Reba Rambo-McGuire and Judy A. Gossett
- *Forever and Ever, Amen* for Paul Overstreet

✳ *GOD101* for Kurt Langstraat
- *How to Receive and Keep Your Healing* for Robert Tilton
- *If Nobody Reaches, Nobody Gets Touched* for Don Gossett
- *In Him* for Randy Gilbert

✳ *Made For More Workbook* for Frank Colacurcio
- *Mark My Words* for Reinhard Bonnke
- *The Mark of the King* for Garth McFadden
- *My Knight In Shining Armor* for Linda Knight
✳ *Restoration Conference Workbook* for Frank Colacurcio
- *Solutions* for Sarah Bowling
✳ *Sowing the Seeds of God* for Steve

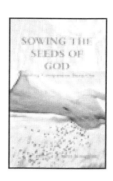

Scroggins
* *Summit Dancer* for Reba Rambo-McGuire
• *Take Your Freedom* for Rita Lecours
* *365 Days* for Frank Colacurcio
* *365 Days Journals #1, 2, 3, and 4* for Frank Colacurcio
• *Training the Human Spirit* for Rogé Abergel
• *Unlimited Potential In Christ* for Kim O. Ryan
• *Win the Lost At Any Cost: The Danny Ost Story* with Harald Bredesen

Also, *The Carpathian Gambit* for Steve Watt, a historical fiction novel.

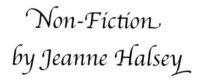

Non-Fiction
by Jeanne Halsey

* *Behold the Lamb* (an Easter Bible Study) Contrary to popular (secular) opinion, I believe the most important season of the Christian calendar is not Christmas, but Easter. While it is wonderful to enjoy the festivities surrounding the birth of Jesus Christ, there is so much more richness and significance in the last days of His ministry and the importance of His death and resurrection – yet much of this joy is overlooked.

* *e-Jeanne: 2003* Once upon a time (okay, early in 2000), I began assembling my random musings (later known as "e-Editorials"), cutting-and-pasting articles that interested me, compiling jokes I thought were funny, and then – almost on a daily basis – joyfully spamming my family and friends through e-mail. This precursor to now-popular blogs was modestly called *e-Jeanne ...*

* *e-Jeanne: 2004 - Part One (January through July)*
"Once I got started, I couldn't stop." The history of *e-Jeanne* began around 1999, really ramped up when 9/11 hit our nation, became more organized and intentional thereafter, and continued until ... 2005? ... *e-Jeanne* was assembled early in the morning (right after my morning devotions – in fact, I realize many of my morning

devotions somehow crept into the e-Editorials), and then forwarded by e-mail to over 300 people all around the world. I did this two or three days a week for 10 years. Like I said, maybe I am a little crazy ...

✳ *e-Jeanne: 2004 - Part Two (August through December)* 2004 was a lengthy year, filled with commentary about the impending American Presidential Election (yes, George W. Bush won again), fluctuating health issues, and much sharing of prayer requests and praise reports among the faithful and beloved Readers. 2004 was so long that I had to split it into two books. Like its sister books, *e-Jeanne: 2004 (Part Two)* comes out looking like a fair-sized phone book; you'll need strong arms and strong hands to hold it while reading ... and I strongly suggest you have a sturdy bookmark.

✳ *e-Jeanne Remnants: 2002, 2005, 2008* The final installment in the *e-Jeanne* series, *e-Jeanne Remnants: 2002, 2005, 2008* is the adventure of any ordinary North American woman as she lived through a watershed decade. Packed with humor, confrontation, wisdom, silliness, life and death, health and illness – all the normal components of life), Jeanne Halsey's "online journals" made for interesting reading. "A must-read for anyone interested in real life in North America as told by an honest writer." ~ Gloria Edwards

• *Exit the Dragon: Fierce Faith Meets Modern Medicine*
• *Falling Out of the Tower*
• *International Guard: A New Life Group Initiative*

✳ *The Legacy of Writing* An experienced, published writer teaches a Creative Christian Writing Class, using humor, anecdotes and simple facts.

• *Naked With God*

✳ *The Parable of Aurelia* People wonder why Life is so difficult, why it seems we lose more than we gain ... when – despite our best efforts – we are continually diminished by hurts, disappointments, shattered dreams. This parable for the 21st century offers an understanding of why and how God is shaping us for greater purposes than we can even dream!

✴ *Shame-Free* How Christian parents can survive their teenager's crisis pregnancy.

✴ *Stubborn Faith: Celebrating Joyce Gossett* As we commemorated the 20th year of my mother Joyce Gossett's Homegoing, I want to honor her memory and the incredible legacy she left for me and our entire family. I choose to not forget this remarkable woman of God who changed the world because of her stubborn faith in Jesus Christ.

✴ *Three Strikes: Dealing With Apathy, Ingratitude and Unbelief* Apathy, unbelief and ingratitude are three attitudes threatening the Christian Church and undermining the lives of followers of Christ. This book addresses those three sins and offers Bible answers to overturn these failings and walk fresh and strong in Jesus Christ!

✴ *What's That You Have In Your Hands?*: Fresh air and hope for the weary soul.

Fiction

✴ *A Bible Fantasy For Jude, Ava, Aja, and Hayley* Four modern-day children are magically transported back to Bible days, where they meet – and play with – Jesus Christ in the middle of the Sea of Galilee ... then hear Him teach the "Sermon on the Mount" ... then share their lunch with Him as He "feeds the 5,000." All from the imagination of gifted writer Jeanne Halsey, and partially illustrated by two of her three granddaughters ... who also star in the story!

✳ *A Christmas Fantasy For Jude and Ava* This is not your run-of-the-mill children's Christmas class. Jeanne "Grammy" Halsey loves to tell stories **to** her grandchildren ... and **about** her grandchildren! This fantasy – where Jude and Ava magically travel back in time ... meet a mysterious, sweet lady ... and experience the Birth of Jesus Christ – is a tribute to Aunty Judy Gossett, who left this Earth before either her great-nephew or great-niece were even born.

✳ *And God Created Theatre* Just as Music and Dance have become commonly accepted forms of Worship in today's Christian Church, I believe it is time to rediscover and reclaim the rightful role of Theatre.

• *Anna the Donkey* (a Children's Christmas Bedtime Story)

✳ *Another Chance* (an Easter Drama) How did Simon Peter genuinely feel during the difficult hours between the arrest, trial, death, and then the resurrection of Jesus Christ? Not yet knowing that Jesus was alive once more, how could he – or anyone – ever expect to have *Another Chance?*

✳ *Another Christmas Fantasy For Jude, Ava and Aja* In this sequel to *A Christmas Fantasy for Jude and Ava,* popular writer Jeanne Halsey adds another grandchild to join in an imaginative adventure back to the time of the birth of Jesus Christ, again aided by a mysterious lady who turns out to be their great-aunt Judy Gossett, who died before any of them were born.

• *Bittersweet* (a Novel of King David and his wife Michel)
• *The Blue Vial* (a Children's Science-Fiction Trilogy)

 ✳ *Messiah! Bright Morning Start Stage Play,* with Reba Rambo-McGuire and Dony McGuire, William and Gloria Gaither, and Judy A. Gossett The Three Wise Guys (also known as "the Three Wise Men") bumble across to Bethlehem ... Joseph displays new-father jitters ... and Angels eagerly watch from Heaven to see how it all turns out. *Messiah! Bright Morning Star* is a collaboration between noted playwright Jeanne Halsey and award-winning songwriters Reba Rambo and Dony McGuire – a wonderful, humorous musical play!

- *That Which I Ought to Do* (a Novel of Paul the Apostle)
- *Ya-Ya* (a Novel of Mary of Bethany)

➡ COMING SOON: *Adventures on Noah's Ark with Jude, Ava, Aja, Hayley, and Cousins*